Geographical Information Systems in Urban Archaeology and Urban Planning

A case study of a modern Greek city,
built on top of an ancient city

Helene Simoni

BAR International Series 2812

2016

Published in 2016 by
BAR Publishing, Oxford

BAR International Series 2812

Geographical Information Systems in Urban Archaeology and Urban Planning

ISBN 978 1 4073 1477 8

COVER IMAGE *Potential archaeological surfaces in the City Plan of Patras, Greece based on the excavations during the period 2004–08*

Printed in England

BAR
PUBLISHING

BAR titles are available from:

BAR Publishing
122 Banbury Rd, Oxford, OX2 7BP, UK
EMAIL   info@barpublishing.com
PHONE   +44 (0)1865 310431
FAX   +44 (0)1865 316916
www.barpublishing.com

Contents

Abstract

The book focuses on a contemporary city, in the subsoil of which archaeological layers survive. The discovery of these layers below a functioning urban area is considered by many to mean the end of construction and development. However, it is argued here that the existence of an archaeological substratum under a city actually constitutes a comparative advantage for its development prospects. To this end, the research methedology uses both qualitative and quantitative data, and the City Plan of Patras was selected as a case study.

The initial part of the study is based on a review of archives and bibliography and the conduct of structured interviews with experts. Subsequently, use is made of Geographical Information Systems and statistics to create a database, to process it digitally, to develop predictive models and to highlight the statistical relationship between data derived from city planning and from archaeology.

From the results it is demonstrated that it is possible to construct a model to predict the hypothetical existence of ancient ruins under a city, as well as the hypothetical depth at which they will be located, based on the recording and processing of city planning and archaeological data, which is derived from five consecutive years of excavations, even without knowing or taking into consideration the history of the city. Using archaeological parameters in combination with city planning data, it is possible to construct specialised models which can highlight the implications of the archaeological foundations of a city for its current functioning and the significance of building regulations.

These results can be used both on an operational level, in the monitoring of construction activity in the city, and as a contribution to a wider investigation of the role of cultural heritage in the planning and promotion of the contemporary city.

Acknowledgements

This book constitutes part of my doctoral thesis which was prepared at the Department of Architecture of the University of Patras and was defended in 2013.

At the outset of this 'journey' I was warned that it would be a lonely one. I resented those words and I set about proving them wrong. Fortunately, my friends, colleagues, professors and especially my family constantly stood by me and supported me, thus rendering my endeavour considerably easier.

I thank my colleagues at the University of Patras and particularly the staff of the Department of Architecture as well as that of the Library and Information Centre.

The material which was used to develop the application of the model for the management of archaeological information in Patras originated from excavations and archaeological research in areas under the supervision of the archaeologist Lambrini Papakosta of the 6th Directorate of Prehistoric and Classical Antiquities (the 6th DPCA). I thank her for her friendly attitude and the opportunity which she gave me to apply my proposals to very interesting material. I also thank Z. Aslamantzidou, the former Director of the 6th DPCA, for unrestricted access to the Directorate's archives and library, as well as all the staff of the service, particularly the warden D. Evaggeliou, who was the main author of the majority of the reports which I studied, and E. Politikou, A. Varelas, E. Argyrou and S. Kanellakis.

I am grateful for the fruitful discussions with Kostas Papagiannopoulos, A. Andrinopoulos and E. Andrinopoulou. In particular, I thank Philippos Alevizos, Professor of the University of Patras for an introduction to the 'World of Statistics'.

It would be an oversight not to mention the experts who participated in the structured interviews. They were the archaeologists L. Kolonas (Honorary General Director of Antiquities and Cultural Heritage), M. Petropoulos (Honorary Ephor of Antiquities), M. Georgopoulou Verra (Honorary Ephor of Byzantine Antiquities), L. Papakosta and the engineers S. Kosmas (Deputy Director of the City Planning Department of the Municipality of Patras), T. Delegkos (former Director of City Planning of the Municipality of Patras), E. Alexopoulou (Director of City Planning of the Municipality of Patras), S. Stamatiou Konstas (topographer of the Directorate of City Planning of the Municipality of Patras), C. Papadatou Giannopoulou (freelance architect), C. Dionysopoulou (freelance architect), A. Pantazis (freelance architect and urban planner), V. Despoiniadou (Lecturer at the Department of Civil Engineering of the University of Patras).

I would like to give a special mention to the members of my supervising committee, Prof. Vassilis Pappas, Prof. Nicos Polydorides, and Prof. Antikleia Moundrea Agrafioti. Prof. Pappas was my chief supervisor and I was very lucky to be guided by him as he was always patient, available and insightful throughout my time as his student.

This book became reality thanks to the encouragement of Prof. John Bintliff, who has been a constant source of inspiration since my first years as a student. I also thank Philip Lauder for the translation of the text from Greek to English and, of course, BAR Publishing, who afforded me a warm welcome to their publications.

However, my greatest debt of gratitude is owed to my family, and it is to them that this book is dedicated, as is everything I do.

Finally, the 'journey' which I undertook was not lonely in the slightest, except for one aspect. I bear full responsibility for the opinions which are expressed in the thesis and the errors which exist are all mine.

Helene Simoni

Chapter 1

Introduction

This book is about a modern city, built over one or more ancient cities which have left traces below contemporary ground level. The modern city spreads and develops through construction works which contribute to the economic and social development of its inhabitants, both individually and collectively. The discovery of ancient phases below a functioning urban area is considered by many to mean the end of construction and therefore of development.

However, the existence of a rich archaeological substratum below a contemporary city constitutes a comparative advantage for its developmental prospects. The archaeological remains, that is the material testimony to human existence in the area over the centuries, represent a part of cultural heritage. The remains themselves constitute a cultural commodity, which is protected for the sake of both historical and contemporary memory, as well as that of the generations to come, and to upgrade the cultural environment.

For example, within the context of the protection and management of the underlying cultural heritage in a contemporary Greek city, all the construction work which requires ground disturbance is checked for the discovery of ancient remains. If none are found, the construction work continues. However, if ancient remains are actually found, the construction activity is interrupted, the Archaeological Service takes possession of the building site and a rescue excavation is carried out, after which work at the building site can be continued under conditions set by the Archaeological Service.

It should be stressed that the terms 'excavation' and 'rescue excavation' are absolutely distinct as they are used in this text. The former refers to all kinds of disturbance of the surface and the removal of soil, whereas the latter refers to the systematic and methodological removal of layers of earth to locate and record archaeological finds (Renfrew & Bahn, 1991: 90-93). Bearing this distinction in mind, for the requirements of this text the term 'archaeological excavation' is used to describe the situation where ancient remains are discovered during the removal of earth in an excavation. In contrast, a 'non-archaeological excavation' is considered to be any excavation in which ancient remains are not found and it is not subsequently required to conduct a rescue excavation.

It is a fact that the current legislative context, though appearing to be simple and clear, proves to be complicated and slow in practice. Archaeologists have difficulty in conducting archaeological research unimpeded, city planners cannot implement their original plan due to archaeological research, and citizens are not easily convinced that what is happening in their city, in their neighbourhood, or on their building site is happening for their benefit (Bakirtzis, 2004). The appearance of the dilemmas which are caused by cultural heritage management is not restricted to one city or one country. It concerns the majority of European countries, which are inspired by a common spirit of faith in the value of protecting archaeological heritage and their development strategies are based on construction projects, mainly large public works (Bozoki Ernyey, 2007a). Examples abound in numerous European cities (Orbasli, 2000; Pickard, 2001).

In Greek cities there are many unresolved cases of archaeological sites found on building sites. Despite the passage of many years or even decades, the local community, the local authority and the central government get caught up in a web of administrative confusion, (Philippides, 2005: 54), thus delaying the management of the antiquities and the development of the site. Such matters are only resolved when the integration of ancient remains into the modern city plan constitutes the honest desire of both private and public stakeholders. In other words, when those involved have been convinced that the harmonious coexistence of the different eras is to their mutual benefit (Sakellaridou, 1999: 19).

A change in mentality and the adoption of viable practices requires the search for and planning of alternative solutions, both in archaeological research and cultural heritage management, as well as the complete integration of its data into city planning. The compilation of up-to-date lists of monuments and potential archaeological sites, in conjunction with the restriction of rescue excavations are actions in this direction. Thus, in this book it is proposed that such action be taken, in combination with the adoption of new methodological tools and the acquisition of skills based on available technology and their innovative utilisation.

The recourse of archaeologists and those managing cultural heritage to technology and particularly computer applications is nothing new. Since the early post-war years the changes that have been taking place in the sociopolitical environment of the West have caused technology to play a key role in all areas of life. Interdisciplinary collaboration between mathematicians and archaeologists with the aim of developing statistical techniques and tests represents the first contribution to the introduction of the methods of the positive sciences into archaeology (Aldenderfer, 1998:

94). With the passage of time, Geographical Information Systems (GIS) have assumed a central position among computer applications which attract the attention of archaeologists and those who deal with cultural heritage management in Europe and North America. GIS has given scientists the ability to work using statistics and automated cartography in their research, combining maps with their databases, creating three-dimensional representations of the terrain, processing satellite images, and creating simulations and models.

In particular, the possibility of predicting potential archaeological sites which are threatened by contemporary construction work makes predictive modelling the most suitable method of managing archaeological assets (Westcott & Brandon, 2000; Mehrer & Westcott, 2006). However, the applications of GIS in urban archaeology have always been limited both in terms of number and extent, since the few examples were usually limited to the study of historical centres and cities (Bigliardi, 2007; Amores et al 2000).

On this theoretical basis a change of course regarding the way in which cultural heritage is dealt with by city planning is deemed to be worthwhile, in order for archaeological research to constitute an essential part of the city planning procedure.

To achieve this aim, an innovative use of tried and tested approaches is proposed, such as: a) some methods of landscape archaeology in archaeological research within the city plan, b) the utilisation of available sources of information which have not been the subject of study to date, such as excavation reports and c) the undertaking of interdisciplinary applications with respect for the existing institutional framework. The originality of this proposal lies in the fact that simple steps can renew and develop the position of archaeological prospecting as a part of the city planning/construction procedure, and improve the relationship between inhabitants and their city, its present and its history.

In order to implement these proposals and to formulate a specific model of cooperation and management regarding city planning activity and archaeological work, the city of Patras in Greece has been selected and, specifically, an area of 2,270 hectares which the approved City Plan of Patras contains. The knowledge of archaeological and city-planning data of the chosen area originates from a review of the bibliography and archives (Rizakis & Petropoulos, 2005; Lambropoulou & Moutzali, 2005; Koumousi Vgenopoulou, 2006; Papadatou Giannopoulou, 1991) but also from the recording of the accumulated experience of experts (researchers and practitioners) who are involved now, or have been so in the recent past, in the planning of the city and/or archaeological research in the city. This experience is recorded in a series of structured interviews with a common questionnaire.

The research questions which were investigated are the following:

1. Is it feasible to utilise basic archaeological data to predict the potential existence of ancient ruins where we are unaware of them?
2. How can a prediction be assessed quantitatively and qualitatively in order to determine its reliability?
3. If the archaeological data is combined with the existing city planning data, can the conclusions that are drawn be integrated into the procedure of city planning and enrich it in such a way as to serve the needs of the inhabitants and to fulfil the commitments of the state?

1.1 Structure of the book

The book will focus on a detailed presentation of the available technological background which can be used as a cutting-edge tool in the management of archaeological inheritance and city planning.

In the chapter which follows a survey is conducted of the uses of different types of quantitative analysis and computer applications. The presentation focuses on GIS and how it can contribute in a unique way to the management of complex databases, to spatial analysis and to the production of new data, in particular, the creation of predictive models of potential archaeological sites. The chapter is mostly dedicated to GIS applications in the city; applications which, to date, have not been particularly highlighted or developed and yet, for precisely that reason, have great potential for an innovative approach and action.

In the third chapter the methodology which will subsequently be followed to investigate the research questions is presented. Thus the ground is prepared for the development and application of a model for the management of archaeological data in city planning and the expected results are given.

The following two chapters present the development and application of a model for the management of archaeological data in city planning. The case study includes the approved Patras City Plan area and the excavation works during the period 1/1/2004-31/12/2008. Subsequently, the specific methodological steps which will be followed are defined. The research has two dimensions: qualitative and quantitative. In Chapter 4 the conclusions of the qualitative research are presented, as they arise from the review of the literature and interviews with experts and practitioners of the related disciplines.

In Chapter 5 the different stages of the quantitative research are presented. The application is based on the creation of a database, the digital processing of the data for the generation of new data and the development of a predictive model. There is also an analytical description of the method of data collection and the method of sample selection, its subsequent digitisation and the structure of the database. Furthermore, the tools of spatial analysis and the statistical processing used are discussed.

Following this a series of GIS applications are presented, including the testing of the distribution of the sample, the construction of maps of potential archaeological sites in the city using Thiessen polygons, the testing of the spatial autocorrelation of various parameters and the construction of a map of probable depth without archaeological deposits in the city with the use of the Kriging method.

Each quantitative analysis is accompanied by a qualitative interpretation of the results and a comparison of my conclusions with the conclusions of past archaeological prospecting in the city, as known from the bibliography. Besides, in this way it is possible to evaluate the utility of the sample which is used and which originates exclusively from the data of a five-year period.

The application is completed with a series of statistical tests to search for relationships between variables which concern the archaeological data and the most important building regulations, such as the floor area ratio, the maximum permitted height and the maximum permitted coverage. At this point other important construction parameters are examined, such as the depth of excavation.

In the conclusion of the book the most important points of the research are highlighted, the basic conclusions are summarised, and adaptations to city planning legislation are proposed, with the introduction of a new building regulation, the maximum permitted depth of excavation.

The book closes with the bibliography and the appendix, where the statistical tests which were conducted for the needs of the fifth chapter are presented.

Chapter 2

GIS as the Technological Background
for the Study of a City

Many of the positions and proposals which are presented in the following chapters are suggested bearing in mind the exceptionally useful contribution of the constantly developing technology of computer science. The fact that digital applications have, to date, only been used on rare occasions to manage the subterranean cultural heritage of the city necessitates an in-depth understanding of the possibilities which these applications offer in order for people to understand and be convinced of their utility.

Such applications were developed principally in the countryside of North America and certain European countries before they spread further afield. They began as analyses of quantitative content and as simple statistical tests. Their users experimented constantly and processed different kinds of spatial data, thus arriving at the generation of advanced predictive models.

In the next section the following questions will be addressed: how was this development connected to the wider sociopolitical context in the West and which research questions was it called on to answer over the course of time? More specifically, how does this theoretical environment operate for GIS, which is gradually assuming a dominant position in the management of information, the production of new information and the construction of models? Finally, interest is focused on what the employment of GIS can provide for the study of cities and how it has been used in different cities to date.

2.1 Archaeology and quantitative analyses

Why did researchers in archaeology first turn to modern technology and mathematical analyses? The use of qualitative methods of analysis of archaeological data has existed for a long time, though at a simple level, and goes back to the 1950ss. Studies, such as the collaboration between a mathematician and an archaeologist (Robinson, 1951; Brainerd, 1951), aimed at developing statistical techniques to create chronological ordering of types of pottery, and Spaulding's (1953), who used statistics to distinguish artefact types, represent the first contributions to the adoption of scientific methods by archaeology. To these can also be added the methods of radiocarbon dating, which are also based on the extensive use of statistics (Doran & Hodson, 1975: 4). Since then archaeologists, in collaboration with experts in physical sciences or alone, have created new trends in their field, initially using very simple applications involving straightforward mathematics.

This development was related to the wider sociopolitical context in the West at that time and the role which technology and history were called on to play in postwar life. The states which emerged stronger from the war and those which were defeated consisted of citizens who had suffered and had been sacrificed and did not wish to relive the experience. The effect of mass destruction which surprised both victors and vanquished was on a larger scale and more powerful than ever before thanks to the media, which brought horrific images before the eyes of millions of people throughout the world. The repugnance and guilt which were caused by the war and the awe of the amazing and terrifying achievements of technology and the physical sciences which were exhibited on all the battlefields led the people of the West to new quests. Thus the nationalistic obsession which caused so much suffering gave way to positivism (Dertilis, 1996:30). In an attempt to heal the wounds of the war the Westerners resorted to an 'antiseptic objectivity' (Diaz-Andreu & Champion, 1996:11), which would not cause offence to anyone. Everything could be interpreted with the aid of mathematics and statistics as quantitative expressions, measurable in an objective and undeniable way. This was intensified by the rapid development of technology which took place from then on and the accessibilty to education and research for ever more people (Clarke, 1973: 8; Hodder, 1993: 18).

In the 1960s archaeologists and anthropologists from North America changed the way in which they posed their research questions and the method of solving them (Binford & Binford, 1968). The movement was called 'Processual' or 'New' Archaeology. Wissler had coined the term 'Real' or 'New' Archaeology in 1917, when he proposed a new research programme based on the resolution of a problem by means of the method of hypothesis and testing, at a time when the principal aim of the traditional methodology was the collection of ancient objects (Wylie, 1993: 20). In the 1960s New Archaeology introduced the deductive method of formulating a hypothesis and testing it, adopting from the outset scientificity and objectivity, precision and rationalism, principles which were better served with the use of mathematics and computers (Shennan, 1988: 8; Doran & Hodson, 1975: 5; Patterson, 1990:190).

The solutions which they chose lent themselves to the use of quantitative analysis, for example, sampling, inventories, the analysis of variables dependent on certain stable factors and settlement patterns (Anschuetz et al 2001: 170). The result was that emphasis was placed mainly on spatial analysis, borrowing methods from anthropogeography (Hodder & Orton, 1976; Aldenderfer, 1998: 101-102). Technically this type of method benefited from the use of aerial photography, which had already been established in World War One and enabled the observation of spatial phenomena on a large scale. A greater boost was given by the introduction of satellite imagery after the launching of LANDSAT in 1972.

The study of the relationship between human groups and the environment, whether natural or man-made, in other words, the subject of anthropogeography, (Derruau, 1987: 13 f.f.), was not new at that time. Since the 19th century it had occupied scientists along with the burning issue of the evolution of the species and the theory which Darwin had recently formulated.

Ratzel represents the German school, which claimed that the environment always influences humankind. In fact, he recognised categories of environmental specifications for the development of particular types of people, e.g. inhabitants of coastal regions, inhabitants of mountainous areas, etc. The idea was that if we compare peoples which are different but which live in similar geographical conditions, any similarities between them will be due to the environment and not to their race (van Dyke Robinson, 1912: 338).

On the other hand, the French School is represented by the circle of the geographer Paul Vidal de la Blache, also an adherent of the idea of the contribution of the environment to the evolution of societies, albeit with some differences. For Vidal and the advocates of the 'School of Possibilism' nature is not a neutral entity which controls human life, but is also profoundly transformed by humans themselves, and subjugated to the extent to which they are able to achieve this. However, natural phenomena do not exert a blind effect on humans. The final choices which a society makes arise from the needs of its members and the available technology (de Blij, 1995: 257) and one can speak only of estimates and possibilities based on some form of statistical analysis of data derived from human observation (Koutsopoulos, 2000: 27, 29).

Vidal's school, though geographical, gave birth to the Annales School a few years later (Dosse, 1993: 32). In 1929 the journal Annales was founded in France, which, as its title states, constitutes: '*Annals of economic and social history*'. During the first post-war years the journal was marked by the presence and contribution of Ferdinand Braudel. Key concepts include generalisation, interdisciplinarity and the use of statistics to utilise measurable data which can lead to arithmetical conclusions (Bintliff, 1991: 5). Braudel introduced the need to study 'immovable history' in the long term in order to understand history in the short term, that is, the history of events. Influenced by Braudel, the 'New' archaeologists of the 1960s went on to conduct regional research on the level of landscape and to use quantitative applications.

In the more recent past, the visualisation of observations, in other words, the ability to explore data using images and graphics, played a major role in continuing their use, even when archaeological theorists introduced 'Post-processual Archaeology', as a reaction to 'New Archaeology' and its principles.

The 'Post-processualists', like Hodder, Tilley and others, claimed that it is not possible to ensure objectivity and accuracy in the interpretation of the past, because this interpretation takes place in the present and therefore exists in the present (Fleming, 2006: 268). Moreover, the choices of people in the past do not always allow interpretation with rational criteria like economic ones, because their choices depend on non-rational values, which are equally important, but which were ignored by the 'New' archaeologists (Shanks & Tilley, 1994:51; Yoffee & Sherratt, 1993:7). Nevertheless, the 'Post-processualists' used and still use mathematical, statistical and computer applications extensively in order to formulate their theories. In this way, they demonstrate that applications of this type are not restricted by theoretical approaches but only by the limits of technology and available software packages.

Computer technology had and still has innumerable applications in archaeological research, communications and education, which has made it attractive but without restricting the way in which scholars think; on the contrary, it has opened up new fields of thought and applications. More importantly, its constantly developing character still makes scholars comment on computational archaeology as an emerging field (Huggett, 2013). Examples can be found in the proceedings of the annual world CAA conference on 'Computer Applications and Quantitative Methods in Archaeology', which celebrated its 40th anniversary in 2012 (http://proceedings.caaconference.org).

An indirect result of this development in the use of technology was the refutation of the ambitious arguments regarding objectivity which would accompany mathematics and computers and would 'protect' the 'unprotected' past from those who would attack or exploit it at will (Hroch, 1996: 299). However, this never happened, as demonstrated by the example of nationalism, which did not disappear. From time to time, it gave way to other values, such as the materialism of the 1970s and the transformation of culture into the Disneyland-type entertainment industry of the 1980s and 1990s (Hodder, 1993: 18). Later, nationalism rose again, as is also happening today, in a globalised, interdependent space (Dertilis, 1996: 33; Kritikos, 2007: 390-394). In this context interest is being rekindled in historical matters and archaeology is used, because its finds are very old, tangible objects which are older than literary evidence (Diaz-Andreu & Champion, 1996: 19-20; Yialouri, 2010: 349).

The shift which took place after the war in the attitude towards the natural sciences encouraged the development of quantitative analysis and especially the adoption of computers. In particular, space technology gave another dimension to the study of geographical/spatial information, and therefore to that of data from archaeology as well as city planning.

2.2 GIS in archaeology and archaeological resource management

How was the connection between the new technology and the analysis of spatial phenomena and the processing of spatial data achieved? From the first Geographical Information System (GIS), which appeared in the middle of the 1960s, the CGIS, commissioned by the Canada Land Inventory (Tomlinson et al 1976), until the appearance of GIS applications in archaeology, about fifteen years elapsed. During this period, however, there were already some archaeologists, mainly in North America, who employed applications with the use of mathematics, statistics and automated cartography in their research. They were juggling different levels of difficulty, combining maps with databases, mapping the results of their statistical analyses, creating three-dimensional representations of the terrain, processing satellite images, and constructing simulations and models (Kvamme, 1995: 2; Kvamme, 1999: 154-155).

The first GIS applications in archaeology date to the end of 1970s (Brown & Rubin, 1982; Chadwick, 1978; Chadwick, 1979) and were pioneering, despite the fact that nowhere in the related publications is any reference made to the term 'Geographical Information System', which had not yet been widely adopted. Brown and Rubin worked in the southwestern U.S.A. Chadwick, a specialist in Mycenaean archaeology, developed, following the 'processual' approach, a simulation of Late Helladic settlement growth as compared to the Middle Helladic settlement pattern (Renfrew & Bahn, 1991: 423).

The impetus towards the more widespread use of GIS was given by the availability on the market of software packages in the 1980s, because, up to that point, scientists had been obliged to write the programs which they used themselves (Marble, 1990:13). The first isolated papers were presented at American archaeological conferences in 1985 and 1986, while at the already established CAA in Britain, which had not yet acquired its international character, there were one or two papers in 1986 and 1987 (Harris & Lock, 1990: 35).

Since then, the use of GIS has spread on both sides of the Atlantic, leading to considerable development and prospects for future evolution in the area of electronic applications in archaeology. They are now considered almost synonymous with Spatial Analysis and one of the pillars of Spatial Technology in archaeology, together with Remote Sensing, Laser Mapping and Geophysical Surveying, although it is not certain that the latter can be used independently without some resort to GIS (McCoy & Ladefoged, 2009). In addition, although their use began by systematising and improving applications which had earlier been used in more 'primitive' and simplistic ways, it succeeded in revolutionising the way in which specialists think about and approach archaeological phenomena.

2.2.1 Database management

The data, in other words, the information which researchers gather during fieldwork, in a laboratory or in a library, traditionally constituted a very large concentrated body in notebooks, rough paper, etc. The use of computers, however, has enabled information to be stored, recorded, recovered and exchanged in a cheap, flexible and rapid way.

In order for data to be incorporated and manipulated in a GIS environment, its spatial character is essential. The rapid increase in the rate of gathering of spatial information in recent years in areas such as geomorphology, geology, hydrology, archaeology, networks, regional planning, city planning and others have created databases with spatial information. The creation of a well organised and standardised database with established criteria can prove to be the most laborious stage of a study.

The database has been likened to a symphony. It consists of many instruments and each one plays its part or a variation on a common theme, the result though being harmonious (Zubrow & Green, 1990: 130). The achievement of harmony in a database is difficult due to the plethora of different parameters involved. This means that different researchers at different moments in time and with diverse criteria as well as knowledge of recording and dating contribute to its development. Fisher (1994: 26 f.f.) summarises the particular characteristics of the data which anthropologists collect as the following: a) it is in notes written in chronological order rather than by topic, does not have a uniform structure and includes many different topics, b) investment in data collection realises most of its expectations and value with the passage of time and after the data has been reorganised and processed in different ways and from various perspectives, c) anthropologists rarely conduct experiments because of ethical, financial or practical difficulties. Their data is collected passively without there always being the possibility of conducting systematic research sampling and d) the data depends on the researchers themselves to be located, collected in a satisfactory way and evaluated. Moreover, researchers have the intellectual capacity to create complex patterns from their data, without needing to formulate it (Fisher, 1994: 28-29).

Of course, this is not only a problem for the humanistic studies. In most cases where a database is kept, there are difficulties with having an officially expressed way of classifying and standardising the finds and observations which arise from archaeological research, particularly when they fail to take into consideration the future use of a GIS in the selection criteria. This involves the danger of recording only that which is uncontroversial and easily mapped. In practice the result is the existence of many small and highly individualised databases in which is stored a huge body of fragmented and unconnected information.

Arroyo-Bishop and Lantada Zarzosa (1995:43-44) refer to the spirit of interdisciplinary cooperation which governs archaeology and stress that the next challenge will be the development and standardisation of a basic method of recording and storing data, if archaeology wishes to enter the world of computers without the coexistence of myriad databases, each one of which can be used only by a limited number of people. For that reason a general concern among all researchers is the existence of databases and a standardised method of filling them at a collective, global (Doerr & Iorizzo, 2008) or at least national level, something which they have been attempting to achieve for years and is now required by law, but has never been completed due to the overaccumulation of material and other stumbling blocks such as underfunding (Malakasioti, 2004: 436).

One benefit, but maybe the most revealing, is the impressive potential for visualising spatial data. It is generally accepted that the human eye has the perceptive ability to process information more quickly from a picture which is seen, than the human mind can process the information which comes from a text which is read (Hearnshaw, 1994). Indeed, more can be said with a map than with words and more information about the spatial distribution of phenomena can be conceived than by the human mind. In many archaeological studies researchers were motivated to adopt GIS by the initial incentive of being able to visualise a large amount of data which had been collected up till then (Simoni & Papagiannopoulos, 1998; Gillings & Sbonias, 1999: 39). The direct and interactive nature of the map offers researchers the maximum from the existing information and an opportunity to tour the landscape with archaeological sites, in such a way that they can approach them visually from whatever perspective and in as much detail as they wish or with as many combinations of data as necessary (McCoy & Ladefoged, 2009: 265). Furthermore, mistakes at the stage of collection and recording become immediately obvious (Wheatley & Gillings, 2002: 83), new correlations are discovered, and decision making regarding the continuation of the methodology or its adaptation is facilitated or accelerated (Kvamme, 1999:160).

Further advantages of visualisation are that it facilitates exchanges among researchers, communication within the scientific community and with the general public (Al-Kodmany, 1999), decision making, the enhancement of education at all levels and of all types (Simoni & Papagiannopoulos, 2001), and the presentation of themes at museums, at exhibitions and on the Internet (Richards, 1998: 340, 342).

Naturally, visualisation is not useful only for the visual observation of data. Often, the eye deceives us and creates relationships which we think exist, but do not, or the opposite. In that case different management of the visualised information is required which the GIS is in a position to provide through simple but more advanced functions (Harris & Lock, 1990; Kvamme, 1993; Syllaios et al 2007: 147).

2.2.2 Spatial analysis – Generating new information

The simplest of the specialised functions which are allowed by the incorporation of a spatial database into a GIS is the generation of descriptive statistics. In this process, however, is taken into consideration not only the geographical position of the data but also the topological relationship between them on the cartographic layer where they belong. Thus it can be seen that it is possible to conduct a wide variety of calculations which describe not only the characteristics of data (variables) but also the relationships between the variables. In this way, the mean, median, maximum, minimum, dispersion and standard deviation of the data can be calculated on every cartographic layer (Haining, 2003: 182). The data can be transformed through arithmetical, trigonometric, logarithmic or logical calculations to be presented in histograms and to be reclassified. In addition, calculations of dimensions (height, area), distance and connectivity, characterisations of proximity, the creation of 'zones' and the identification of clusters can be carried out (Conolly & Lake, 2006: 112; Syllaios et al 2007: 149-156).

The more complex the functions which are attempted, the more necessary it becomes to check the statistical significance of their results. Spatial statistics is proposed exactly because, as demonstrated by its definition, it corrects the aspatial nature of classical statistics and acts in a complementary fashion to classical tests of significance e.g.: x^2, Kolmogorov-Smirnov, T-test and others. Usually, the identification of spatial patterns is based on the principle that spatial data which are found close to each other are more likely to resemble each other than others which are located at a greater distance. This principle is known as the 'First Law of Geography' (Tobler, 1970).

The most common statistical test is that of spatial autocorrelation, a property which a non-spatial model would be unable to incorporate (Cressie, 1993:24; Schwarz & Mount, 2006: 170-171). It refers to the degree of correlation between a pair of values and the distance between them in the spatial distribution (Cliff & Ord, 1981; Kvamme, 1996: 47). A positive spatial autocorrelation confirms the 'First Law of Geography', while a negative autocorrelation exists in cases where similar values are located far from each other (Conolly & Lake, 2006: 158). In addition, it is possible to test spatial autocorrelation both on a global and a local level. On the global level, the statistical test gives a unique index which is valid for all the area of study and describes the total distribution of the spatial information, while on the local level it enables every case to be examined individually and a table of values to be produced (Premo, 2004:856-7).

The functions of the investigation and analysis of data are not restricted to the limits of one cartographic layer, but are extended to new layers which arise from the superimposition of two or more existing ones. Each new layer is nothing less than new information and a new thematic map. Even the structure of the cartographic layer can be converted, because other uses and certain tasks can be performed using vector data structures and others by raster data structures (Burrough: 1993, 169).

Among the most interesting techniques for producing new information and, naturally, new thematic maps, is interpolation. With this method it is possible to predict the value of a variable in all the points in a space for which there are no measurements or observations, using sample measurements or observations which have already taken place in the same space (Burrough & McDonnel, 1998:98). A characteristic of interpolation is that it can be applied to two types of data, qualitative and quantitative, with the choice of the appropriate technique and this advantage, together with the development of various techniques, has established interpolation as one of the most used methods of GIS (Beex, 2004; Burrough & McDonnel, 1998: 98 f.f.).

The most obvious use is the creation of a digital elevation model, which represents the relief of the Earth. However, because all types of data can be chosen, users are given the opportunity to represent whatever view of the 'real world' they wish, with variables selected from the natural environment (slopes, orientation, drainage, etc.) or from human intervention (administrative districts, hierarchical structures, archaeological layers, land uses, etc.) (Kvamme, 1990a; Gaffney & Stančič, 1991).

Since the values or observations which are predicted by the process of interpolation are not real, but are the mathematically best estimates, it is always necessary to be able to assess the reliability of the model and, where different techniques of interpolation are applied, which one is the most suitable. The ability to test the accuracy of the results of predictive models is the strongest selection criterion. The test can be conducted either with new samples or by means of internal tests on the existing sample and is carried out in the form of a statistical analysis of the results. In the latter case, the user may evaluate the performance of each technique in order to decide whether and if so which of the techniques adopted produced statistically significant results and which of all produced the best (Verhagen, 2009; Robinson & Zubrow, 1999; Peña et al 1999: 42; Farinetti & Sigalos, 2002; Verhoeven & Vermeulen, 2004).

2.2.3 Predictive modelling

One of the most powerful tools which GIS offers in the service of cultural heritage management is the predictive model. The construction of predictive models using GIS is the most widespread method of locating, testing and predicting spatial information including archaeological information. The numerous applications which have been performed since the end of the 1970s when they were first used until today demonstrate this fact (Kvamme, 1983; Kohler & Parker, 1986; Warren et al 1987; Kvamme, 1989; Allen et al 1990; van Leusen, 1996; Stančič & Kvamme, 1999; Westcott & Brandon, 2000; Mehrer & Westcott,

2006; Kantner, 2008: 51-52; Rua, 2009; Graves, 2011 and many more…).

From time to time two different approaches in the construction of predictive models have been adopted, the explanatory-deductive and the inductive-correlative. According to the former approach, the researcher formulates a theoretical hypothesis to investigate the distribution of archaeological sites in a space, constructs the model and then tests its effectiveness on known archaeological sites in that space. If the model is successful, then it can be used to search for unknown sites in the same area, to which the prerequisites of the initial theory apply (Church et al 2000: 146-147; Kamermans, 2006).

The inductive-correlative approach is more usual, but follows the opposite route. The inductive models are based on the acknowledgement that analysing the data from known archaeological sites can define the factors which have influenced the distribution of those sites in the area. Once these factors have been identified, it is then possible to estimate the type and extent of the contribution of each factor in identifying an archaeological site. This knowledge enables the location of potential new sites in unexplored parts of the wider area and in positions where the same factors apply (Veljanovski and Stančič, 2006; Ebert, 2000).

The usual factors which are used to determine the useful parameters of a predictive model are those which are related to the environment. Altitude, slope, orientation, distance from water and geology are by far the most common building blocks of a model of potential archaeological sites. The insistence on these factors has led the reliability of these models to be criticised for being environmentally deterministic. Given the lack of studies of past geography, these factors reflect the contemporary form of the environment and not that of the period when the sites were in use. A further accusation is that the use of a site at any moment in the past was not dictated exclusively by external environmental conditions, but also by internal mechanisms of the functioning of the group or the individual connected with social, religious or other dynamics (Wilcox, 2013; Wilcox, 2012; Ebert, 2000; Lock & Harris, 2006; van Leusen, 1996: 181-183; Gaffney & van Leusen, 1995; Wheatley, 1993).

Nevertheless, mostly Europeans researchers have also attempted on many occasions to objectify and quantify this subjective character of the so-called social and anthropogenic variables with analyses of visibility, movement within the space and cost surface in order for it be modelled (Paliou et al. 2014).

The ability to predict potential archaeological sites which are under threat from modern construction works makes predictive modelling the most suitable method of managing cultural heritage and this is its fundamental contribution to archaeology (Whitley, 2004). Its use began in America and it took over a decade for it to cross the Atlantic and be applied on European soil. This is testified by the first two books which were published containing articles devoted exclusively to archaeology and GIS, the first written by American researchers about applications from North America (Allen et al 1990), the second written by Europeans, about applications originating from the 'European agenda' (Lock & Stančič, 1995). In the American publication, seven of the eleven articles present applications of predictive modelling, whereas in the European publication, although it was released five years later, there are no applied predictive models. The book contains only one article in which two archaeologists with experience of GIS take it in turns to play the roles of critic and advocate of environmental determinism (Gaffney & van Leusen, 1995; Simoni, 1999).

The United States of America offered the best conditions for the development of predictive modelling due to its vast open spaces under state control (Kvamme, 1995: 3). In this available space American archaeologists had the opportunity to apply such models in order to predict distributions of archaeological resources, to inform investors and to guide them in advance to focus their construction plans on sites where the discovery of ancient remains and their consequent destruction by building work was less likely. An additional benefit was the reconstruction, wherever possible, of the ancient settlement patterns of an area, but also an understanding of the most important environmental criteria for locating archaeological sites (Warren, 1990: 202).

The reason why this method developed and gained popularity earlier on the American continent and much later in Europe was a result as much of the types of archaeology as of the types of cultural management which were developing on the two continents before the 1990s, which was a decisive decade for the Europeans.

In America, the philosophy of spatial management was more incorporated into the obligations of the individual states and the federal government. The characteristic American landscape of vast but uninhabited or sparsely inhabited expanses was the ideal field in which to develop pioneering methods and quantitative applications (Kantner, 2008: 39; Harris & Lock, 1995: 354 f.f.).

In Europe, emphasis is not traditionally placed on the landscape which, in any case, has been fragmented and densely populated since ancient times, but on specific sites and the location of the best ones for archaeological research excavations (van Leusen, 1996: 180). A characteristic obsession of the older archaeologists was with the excavation of archaeological sites with the aim of discovering works of art which would adorn the collections of eccentric wealthy Europeans or the big royal or national museums (Schnapp, 1996). However, apart from serving research purposes, the archaeological excavation constituted the only means of managing archaeological cultural heritage (Bozoki Ernyey, 2007a).

When big development works in Europe in both the country and cities required that measures be taken to protect unknown archaeological remains, predictive modelling proved to be a useful methodological tool. This was achieved with the utilisation of GIS, which, even though it had been developed for other purposes, proved to serve those of archaeological research. The greatest advantage was that it could not only systematise and improve applications which were already in use, but also change the researchers' way of thinking. This took place mainly in landscape archaeology, less so in research excavations and hardly at all in urban archaeology.

2.3 GIS in urban archaeology: Applications and implications

In contrast to the frequent use of GIS applications for the needs of city and land use planning (Stillwell & Clarke, 2004; Diappi, 2004; Laurini, 2001; Stillwell et al 1999; Pappas, 1994), urban archaeological research has not exploited the advantages of GIS. In the first publications (Allen et al 1990; Gaffney & Stančič, 1991; Lock & Stančič, 1995) there are no applications in urban archaeology and the vast majority are in landscape archaeology. This dominance of landscape research in the first steps of archaeological GIS resulted in practitioners neglecting the importance of integrating rescue excavation research into a GIS environment and in its limited use (Moscati, 1999: 103· Wheatley & Gillings, 2002: 235). This is because rescue excavations usually take place in cities, whereas investigations in landscape archaeology rarely do so, as they require open spaces.

The almost exclusive use of GIS in landscape archaeology is due to the ease with which its data can be classified and recorded on a database and mapped compared with data from research excavations, particularly when the latter originates from cities which have been inhabited continuously for centuries (Merlo, 2004: 277-8; Bigliardi, 2007: 98; Wheatley & Gillings, 2002: 235).

The fact is that the first users of GIS in archaeology belonged to the school of New Archaeology, and landscape archaeology did not work well for the traditional rescue excavation archaeologists. The latter considered that the new technological developments did not concern them, and they also lacked familiarity with quantitative analysis and the use of computers. With the passage of time GIS became ever more effective in landscape studies rather than in on-site studies, because demand for the former grew and with it the users' requests for new algorithms and techniques of analysis (Biswell et al 1995: 269; Huggett, 2000: 118; Wheatley & Gillings, 2002: 235). Furthermore, landscape archaeologists showed a great willingness to learn programming and to write their own programs when GIS had not yet been established as a commercial product (Kvamme, 1990a: 123).

2.3.1 GIS on the 'site' scale

In contrast to the theoretical basis of landscape archaeology, which was developed in the same period as when researchers were adopting quantitative methods and the use of computers, the theoretical approach of the rescue excavation had already been formed at the beginning of the twentieth century on the basis of the study of stratigraphy. The aim of the rescue excavation was to detect archaeological layers as they appear in the horizontal and vertical dimensions. Put simply, an archaeological layer is considered to contain all contemporary activity, while the vertical sequence of layers shows the changes in activities through time (Renfrew & Bahn, 1991: 90).

The traditional examination of the horizontal dimension of the stratigraphic unit included its delineation, the recording of finds and the identification of each group of finds (Arroyo-Bishop & Lantada Zarzosa, 1995: 46-47). Even in this case, researchers need to examine their finds in relation to the others found in the same stratigraphic context or in successive ones. This necessitates the special handling of data, which, however, GIS proved incapable of providing, mainly because of the inability to include the chronological dimension in the information (Richards, 1998: 342; Katsianis et al 2008: 656). Due to this disadvantage, GIS could not live up to the expectations of excavators (Wheatley & Gillings, 2002: 235; Harris & Lock, 1995: 355-7; Harris & Lock, 1996: 307). The ease with which GIS handles the almost linear, objective and irreversible perception of time in a landscape study (Katsianis et al 2008: 656) does not seem to have found its equivalent in studies on the scale of the archaeological site (Constantinidis, 2007). Moreover, the reality of a rescue excavation is never as clear and as ideal as it has been described above, that is, as a sequence of layers, each of which extends horizontally exactly above the previous ones and/or below the next ones. It depends on the method which excavators follow to resolve this problem, but also to answer their research questions.

The rescue excavation is a complicated and extremely costly procedure. Due to its slow rate of progress, which is necessitated by the careful approach to what is in any case a destructive action, it is extremely time-consuming. Apart from the unevenness of the stratigraphic units, its complexity is attributed to the human element in the phase of the discovery and recording of data, which results in their quality varying considerably. This becomes even more obvious when, with the passage of time, there is a high turnover of staff conducting and even coordinating the excavation.

Therefore, it is no coincidence that the archaeological excavations which have adopted the use of GIS are mainly systematic studies which take place outside the urban environment and have guaranteed financial support from funds for academic purposes, the training of students or the promotion of research in archaeology and history. Such examples, though few in number, have been presented at scientific conferences and published in journals and concern a variety of sites from different time periods, the Prehistoric (Vullo et al 1999; Katsianis et al 2008; Mantzourani & Vavouranakis, 2003; Barceló et al 2003), Classical Antiquity (Laurenza & Putzolu, 2002; D'Andrea et al 1999; Biswell et al 1995), the Middle Ages (Machácek & Kucera, 2004; Cattani et al 2004) and sites with multiple cultural levels (Csáki et al 1995:88, 90). There are many cases of archaeological excavations that have been completed for many years and later a GIS revises the old data, e.g. at Miletus and Piraeus (Sidiropoulos & Sideris, 2003), at Knossos (Katsianis, 2004) and at Akrotiri (Constantinidis, 2001).

All these archaeological research excavations are conducted within strict academic limits and rarely have anything to do with cultural heritage management. It is no coincidence that of the aforementioned references only in one case had the aim of management been set. The study in question concerned the Italian city of Pontecagnano. Among the stated objectives of the study were, on the one hand, to investigate the ancient settlement and, on the other, to incorporate the data into the city plan (D'Andrea et al 1999: 146). In the other cases the aims reflect the usual GIS applications, that is, the management of a database and its visualisation.

Indeed, almost everyone wants a GIS to achieve visualisation of their data (Csáki et al 1995: 97; Laurenza & Putzolu, 2002; Doneus & Neubauer, 2004; Machácek & Kucera, 2004; Cattani et al 2004; Barceló et al 2003; Katsianis et al 2008; Vullo et al 1999). This allows the use of analytical tools to investigate the spatial distribution of finds and the creation of the stratigraphy (Richards, 1998: 338) and, by extension, the history of the site, although these uses are referred to explicitly by fewer authors (Biswell et al 1995; Csáki et al 1995: 94-95; Machácek & Kucera, 2004; Cattani et al 2004; Barceló et al 2003; Katsianis, 2004; Katsianis et al 2008). However, as a more demanding procedure, this can only be carried out by someone with at least a basic knowledge of spatial statistics. Nevertheless, in some cases the authors hoped to arrive at a predictive model of potential sites in order to schedule future rescue excavations (Vullo et al 1999; Cattani et al 2004; Fronza et al 2001; Fronza et al 2003: 149).

As far as archaeological excavations are concerned authors avoid criticising their methods and effectiveness. They limit themselves to a simple presentation of their work. However, in a few cases where authors have expressed their concerns, the method of excavation itself is considered to be the greatest obstacle (Biswell et al 1995; Katsianis, 2004; Katsianis et al 2008; Vullo et al 1999) and less so other special circumstances, such as low funding or poor quality of old excavational data (Biswell et al 1995; Vullo et al 1999).

In 1999 Kvamme (1999: 164-165) commented that up to that time GIS had been applied on the level of the site in a limited way and were little more than a tool for the two-dimensional management of excavational data. Ten years later a slow but steady improvement in the situation could be observed (McCoy & Ladefoged, 2009: 272). McCoy and Ladefoged find that this change lies in the development of related techniques of conservation, taphonomy, typology and geophysics, rather than in the method of excavation itself. However, during this decade the researchers were also seeking a truly three-dimensional GIS, but with varying degrees of success (Harris & Lock, 1996: 307; Blasco Bosqued et al 1996: 197; Huggett, 2000:120; Avern, 2001:7; Barceló et al 2003: 85; Cattani et al 2004: 299; Fernández & Solé, 2007; Katsianis et al 2008: 666) and always outside the urban space.

2.3.2 GIS on the 'city' scale

As far as purely urban applications of GIS are concerned, in an archaeological but not excavational context, there is a clearly different methodological approach. In nearly all the cases the data originates from older sources of various kinds, cartographic, archival, excavational, narrative, from chance discoveries, from surface finds and whatever else has contributed to existing knowledge over time (Miller, 1995: 320; Amores et al 1999; Amores et al 2000; Guermandi, 1999; Börner, 2001; Börner, 2002; Peskarin, 2002; Mackay & Mackay, 2002; Zinglersen, 2004; Fernández & Solé, 2007; Bigliardi, 2007; Rodier et al 2010). In addition, researchers' ambitions almost always simultaneously serve the purposes of both academic research and cultural heritage management in the context of city planning (Miller, 1995: 320; Guermandi, 1999; Börner, 2001; Börner, 2002; Mackay & Mackay, 2002; Bigliardi, 2007; Blasco Bosqued et al 1996; Baena Preysler et al 1999; Rodier et al 2010).

Certain individual objectives are no different from those of systematic research excavations. In other words, it is deemed useful and meaningful that all of the available and updated information is incorporated into a unified database, with the ability to depict it on a map (Miller, 1996; Amores et al 1999; Amores et al 2000; Guermandi, 1999; Börner, 2001; Börner, 2002; Peskarin, 2002; Mackay & Mackay, 2002; Zinglersen, 2004; Fernández & Solé, 2007; Bigliardi, 2007; Blasco Bosqued et al 1996; Baena Preysler et al 1999; Rodier et al 2010). This advantage, together with the ability to share information with citizens, institutions and companies involved in construction work in the city (Amores et al 1999; Amores et al 2000; Guermandi, 1999; Börner, 2001; Börner, 2002; Mackay & Mackay, 2002; Zinglersen, 2004; Blasco Bosqued et al 1996; Baena Preysler et al 1999; Bigliardi, 2007) represent the most important and popular uses of GIS. In fact fewer than half of the applications connect the management of the archaeological resources of the city with the investigation of the stratigraphy and the construction of models of archaeological deposition (Chartrand et al 1993; Börner, 2001; Börner, 2002; Peskarin, 2002; Mackay & Mackay, 2002; Zinglersen, 2004:). In addition, there are even fewer applications of predictive modelling (Miller, 1996; Börner, 2001 Börner, 2002; Peskarin, 2002; Bigliardi, 2007) and

of planning future research strategies (Amores et al 1999; Amores et al 2000; Zinglersen, 2004; Papadopoulos et al 2009), which, however, are more demanding applications but also more popular among those involved in landscape archaeology.

The limited implementation of these methods in urban archaeology raises the question as to whether applying them actually leads to the realisation of the initial aims. It is often the case that the objectives are much more optimistic and ambitious than a more realistic view of things would justify (Miller, 1996: 370). The insurmountable problems which all cities appear to face are the very inconsistent nature of the information which is recorded in databases, the poor quality of some data, the omission of essential details, the inaccuracy of old maps, the documentation of old rescue excavations, which is inadequate by modern standards, and the lack of metadata (Miller, 1996: 371; Amores et al 1999; Amores et al 2000; Fernández & Solé, 2007; Bigliardi, 2007; Blasco Bosqued et al 1996; Baena Preysler et al 1999).

Apart from the old and obsolete methodologies, it is also worth taking into consideration the weaknesses of the theoretical background, which hinder the adoption of the full potential of a GIS and reduce its use to the simple creation of beautiful maps. For example, there is a tendency to deal with an ancient city as a unified site which extends horizontally below the contemporary city, parts of which have been detected but others remain undiscovered. If, however, the isolated sections of the ancient site are considered to be parts of a whole, then that can serve research and academic purposes in the reconstruction of history, but this does not lead to an understanding of the relationship between the individual sites and also with the excavated but non-archaeological sites in the city. This approach is absolutely non-existent and it appears not to be taken into account, because in a modern city the excavated but non-archaeological sites vastly outnumber the archaeological ones and recording them seems to be wasted effort, thus excluding valuable observations regarding non-archaeological sites from scientific documentation.

The obsession with one archaeological site, in most cases imaginary, which incorporates all the known and excavated sites of the urban fabric, often leads researchers to choose the historical centres of well known cities as an area to study, e.g. Seville (Amores et al 1999: 354-355; Amores et al 2000: 109). But Bigliardi, referring to the historical city of Parma, admits that the choice of historical centres as fields of GIS application proves to be not particularly useful, since it is known that everywhere in the historical centre there is a strong chance of discovering antiquities. An application that is extended geographically throughout the modern city would be preferable (Bigliardi, 2007: 99).

Regarding an application in York a divergence between the 'declarations of the plan' at the start of the investigation (Chartrand et al 1993) and the subsequent report can be observed (Miller, 1996: 371). In the former publication it is stated as an objective to construct a series of models which would represent the morphology of the land in the city during different time periods and, as a result, to construct a general model of the state of the archaeological deposition of the whole city. Three years later, one of the members of the team admitted that, in reality, a large part of the excavational data that was to be taken into consideration was incompatible for recording in the database and further processing for the construction of the desired models. Finally, in the models that were constructed, the division of the deposition into archaeological zones led to zones of an average thickness of two metres, beginning from ground level to 20 metres below the surface since the deposition was exceptionally thick (Miller, 1996). This particular methodology became almost impossible to use in areas with thinner deposits and smaller differences between the layers.

Researchers' dependence on old historical maps of the Spanish city Tarragona had a negative effect on the functioning of a complete model of the Roman colony of Tarraco. The historical maps were initially deemed the most useful means for reconstructing the rich archaeological palimpsest of the city which had been destroyed due to urban expansion and mainly the establishment of quarries in the 19th century. These maps, which date from the 17th century and later, contain information about the topography of the city and the ancient monuments which still existed when they were made. By superimposing one on the other in chronological order and finally on a map of the contemporary city and connecting them all with the available archaeological information about the city, the ancient topography with all its monuments was to be revealed. In practice, the endeavour proved to be very difficult and special processing of the maps was required (Fernández & Solé, 2007: 423).

One recent application of urban geophysical research in a GIS environment appears to be very promising (Papadopoulos et al 2009). Geophysics has been used for a long time in archaeological research (Novaković & Simoni 1999; Papadopoulos et al 2012: 1961) with successful results, mainly in studies in the countryside and in open spaces. Its basic advantage lies in the fact that it constitutes a non-destructive method of detecting, recording and mapping archaeological remains in the subsoil, but without an excavation taking place (Tsokas et al 1994: 98). Furthermore, a combination of different techniques and methods of geophysical surveying reinforces the reliability of the measurements and of the final conclusions regarding the depth, position and extent of potential finds (Diamanti et al 2005: 90; Papadopoulos, 2006: 179). GIS helps interpret geophysical data and compare it with spatial data, by providing all the tools of spatial analysis and of the generation of new information (Vafidis et al 2003).

However, the implementation of equivalent methods and techniques within the modern urban landscape has a number of weaknesses. These are due to the particularly heterogeneous nature of the subsoil layers, the interference

which the measuring instruments are subject to because of electric current and electromagnetic radiation, and even traffic and pedestrians (Papadopoulos, 2009: 56-57). If the exceptionally high cost of these applications and the demands on human resources are also taken into account, it becomes obvious why it is considered to be difficult for this technology to be used outside the academic world, for reasons other than pure research (Diamanti et al 2005: 90).

Nevertheless, one of the most analytical studies in urban geophysical surveying was conducted in Heraklion and Rethymnon by the Institute for Mediterranean Studies (Papadopoulos et al 2009). In order for the researchers to avoid traffic and noise, they were occasionally obliged to work after midnight. Their applications were used in public works, such as the construction of a coastal road in Heraklion and the erection of a cultural centre in the playground of a school. The only privately funded work in which geophysical research was also carried out was on a plot of land belonging to the Institute itself. The results were encouraging, as the potential antiquities were accurately mapped and the excavational activity which followed was limited to the points which had been indicated by the geophysical research, thus confirming the initial conclusions (Papadopoulos et al 2009: 65). It remains, however, to apply this method in more cases, in order to come to a conclusion as to how much its use can be generalised and contribute to the avoidance of rescue excavations in cities.

In Vienna, a database has been established in a GIS environment with all the available archaeological material from rescue excavations in the city and every other available source, with the main aim of protecting the city's cultural heritage by raising public awareness as well as that of the local government. Apart from extensive spatial analysis which is carried out at different sites, predictive maps of potential archaeological layers are created. It is hoped that, in this way, the inhabitants themselves will contribute to the protection of the history of the city, because, as they themselves admit, the archaeologists are unable to be present at all the excavations which are carried out and to locate archaeological sites (Börner, 2001: 152; Börner, 2002). Thus, the confirmation and evaluation of the models which were constructed depend on the inhabitants' motivation.

In Rhodes in 1986 the Historical and Archaeological Institute of the Dodecanese took on the development of GIS for the systematic digital recording and encoding of existing data concerning archaeological research both in the capital and the rest of the island. The initial aim of the application was to facilitate archaeological research, study and final publication in a context which would make the most of the use of technology (Zarifis, 1996; Zarifis, 1998). Cooperation between the Municipality of Rhodes and the Archaeological Service allowed the scope of the research to be broadened. In this way, the archaeological information could be used in the documentation, study and programming of modern city planning interventions in a city which is spreading dynamically over its ancient and mediaeval phases. This could be achieved by constructing a model of the depths at which antiquities and natural earth are expected to be found.

The first problems with the application appeared very early on due to internal and external reasons. On the one hand, the technical support from the company which provided the software was inadequate and, on the other, it proved exceptionally difficult to continuously update the database (Charatzopoulou, 2001: 125). Finally, the applications which came to the attention of the public were connected with the spatial analysis of individual buildings and took place for research purposes (Zarifis & Brokou, 2002). From the moment which the Institute completed the project and handed the program to the Municipality, the application faced the inflexibility which one encounters in many local government services. By 2006 the system had developed all the weaknesses of the 'old systems'. This is because there were no plans for it to be updated and upgraded, it exclusively served purposes within the service, it was deprived of an experienced user devoted to its use and had become non-functional (Gialis et al 2006).

A very optimistic approach has been introduced in Nicosia where a multidisciplinary project has been launched with the aim of establishing good practices for rescue/preventive archaeology and urban planning. The researchers plan to integrate all kinds of data (archaeological, geological, technical, etc.) concerning a building site and to simulate alternative scenarios to prevent archaeological disturbance. The solutions will be highly dependent on a significance analysis of each archaeological excavation, based on criteria such as rarity, chronology, conservation, value, etc. More importantly, the risk level is defined in each case, related to the archaeological potential of the site. What is not clear, though, is the way in which the archaeological potential and any incurred risk will be determined in advance (Hermon & Vassalo, 2012).

In contrast to the aforementioned applications which were implemented in a modern built-up space, in Madrid a surface survey which was carried out on the outskirts of the city aimed to conduct the archaeological documentation of a non-built up space with primary research and the collection of surface archaeological finds before the area was given over to construction activity. Since it adopted a standard method of landscape archaeology, it made use of all the advantages of applied GIS and regional research and was restricted to antiquities up to the Roman period (Blasco Bosqued et al 1996; Baena Preysler et al 1999).

It is clear that, as far as the management of urban archaeology is concerned, the use of GIS is limited to the construction and updating of databases and making maps, which usually depict excavational strata. The theoretical background of urban archaeologists has not allowed them to incorporate the use of such systems in their methodological armoury, and wherever that does take place, practical problems remain to be solved in order for their use to be more widespread.

2.4 Conclusion

The use of quantitative methods of analysis of archaeological data has developed rapidly from the first attempts in the 1950s to the present day. In particular, the use of GIS has enabled the development of new methods of formulating and interpreting archaeological data and has become a prerequisite for its manipulation in the realm of spatial analysis.

GIS allows and requires the construction of databases which are organised and standardised with stable criteria, possess impressive capabilities to represent spatial data and promote the exchange of information. Since GIS functions for investigating and analysing data are not restricted, they can be extended to new cartographic layers and produce new information, the most characteristic example being that of the predictive model.

Despite the wealth of GIS applications in cities for the purposes of city and land use planning, urban archaeology has not yet exploited the advantages of GIS and has not incorporated the whole range of their capabilities into its methodological armoury. This situation, however, can be reversed to change the whole approach of urban archaeology and its management.

Chapter 3

Urban Planning and Urban Archaeology

3.1 Theoretical framework

A common phenomenon in many parts of the world, including Europe, particularly in the south, are modern cities which have been continuously inhabited for centuries or even millenia. The resultant continuous building over the ages was not considered a problem since respect for history was not connected with the preservation of the tangible remains; on the contrary, reconstruction was considered to contribute to the necessary renovation and development of a city, even if it happened in an anarchic and arbitrary way (Hunter, 1981: 26; Yerolympos, 1996: 14).

Indeed, the expansion of cities was connected with economic activity more than any other factor. Continual wars and their devastating consequences for human life and infrastructure which Europeans have experienced, as of course the Greeks have until recently, have led them to use reconstruction as the surest means of achieving economic progress and prosperity (Lambrianides, 2002: 229). In the post-war years the Greek countryside was abandoned and, with the encouragement and/or tacit consent of successive governments, people migrated to the cities to work in factories (Kagkarakis, 2005: 133; Koutsopoulos, 2005: 212; Petrakos & Oikonomou 1999: 22-23), while home ownership became synonymous with financial success, social advancement and a good marriage (Oikonomou, 1988: 74, 102; Oikonomou, 2010: 96). In this context, systematic illegal construction, building outside the city plan and the absence of regional and city planning were considered justified. At the same time, other characteristics became part of the urban way of life, such as constant urbanisation to the detriment of the countryside, the lack of sufficient public spaces, land speculation, the dramatic rise in the popularity of the private car as the main means of transport for long and short journeys, pollution, the breakdown of the social fabric and the loss of collective identity (Lefas, 1985: 128; Liroudias 1995: 16, 90; Oikonomou & Petrakos 1999: 413-417; Oikonomou, 2000: 39, 44; Christophilopoulos, 2002: 24, 450; Vaiou et al 2000; Karydis, 1991: 319; Kydoniatis, 1985: 26; Aravantinos, 1992: 324; Polydorides et al 1985: 19-20).

In the context of intense urbanisation and with the construction sector synonymous with development, the introduction of building regulations was necessary for the imposition of basic conditions and specifications aimed at governing construction and setting limits in relation to other needs and obligations of both citizens and the state (Yerolympos, 2000: 151; Christophilopoulos, 1988: 3). The protection of antiquities encountered in earthmoving works for the foundations of construction work is deemed to be such a need and obligation. Therefore, it is illegal to demolish ancient ruins in order to erect new buildings. The construction of a road, for instance, over antiquities is tantamount to its temporary or total cessation, or even the impossibility of implementing the original plan. The work is automatically interrupted and an archaeological investigation commences. Consequently, from the point of view of construction as a developmental procedure, the presence of antiquities may be considered an inhibitive factor. Nevertheless, city planning rarely takes archaeological information into consideration beforehand and the building regulations of an area are not based on the potential existence of archaeological remains in the subsoil.

The need for the protection of antiquities did not arise suddenly but gradually, when both peoples and rulers realised that the tangible remains of antiquity could be used as symbolic capital to strengthen their position in relation to other states and subsequently to create nation-states (Diaz-Andreu & Champion, 1996: 8; Hroch, 1996: 295; Meskell, 1998). Already by the end of the 19th century laws had been passed in all the countries of Europe to protect archaeological finds as part of their national heritage (Hunter, 1981: 24), whereas since the second half of the 20th century international organisations have signed and member-states have ratified treaties protecting archaeological remains as an inseparable part of the global cultural identity and heritage and as a human right (van Leusen, 1996; Dejeant-Pons, 2006; Dolff Bonekämper, 2009).

In Greece in particular the existing institutional framework for cultural heritage management is constitutionally safeguarded and consists of a considerable body of laws, which cumulatively define the limits between development and the protection of antiquities (Skouris & Trova, 2003). According to this, the definitions of 'archaeological sites' and 'historical places' are not limited to sites where archaeological remains stand. They also include the sites where it is suspected antiquities existed in the past which are connected with mythical or significant historical events, as well as open space around the sites (Law 3028, 2002: Article2§c, d).

Although considerable progress in this direction has actually been made, effective communication between the different partners and even within the public sector itself has yet to be achieved. As a result, on the one hand, the construction sector continues to believe that it loses out due to the intervention of archaeologists and, on the other, archaeologists continue to believe that they are underestimated when their work is ignored in the midst of pressures and conflicts (Bureš, 2007: 26; Thomas, 2007: 40; Gleeson, 2007: 144; Bis Worch, 2007:157; Djurič, 2007: 183; Tsilipakou, 2004: 427-428; Marki, 2004: 437). In this context, more attention is paid to large public works which are mainly regarded as being developmental (Kakouris, 2004a: 451; Mendoni, 2004: 476). In contrast, the contribution of smaller scale private works to the developmental balance sheet of the country is underrated, as if it were forgotten that a large number of small works can occupy a larger space and require considerably more ground disturbance, but also greater expense on the part of the state to pay for an archaeological investigation to be carried out. As a result, private individuals proceed with their construction projects completely ignoring the possibility of the work being erected over antiquities, with all the associated financial, social and scientific consequences (Bureš, 2007: 24; Schauman Lönnqvist, 2007: 52-53; Hjaltalin, 2007: 130; Maggi, 2007: 151).

In addition, cultural heritage management by states and historical cities in general has not succeeded in convincing the public that the inconvenience it causes is worth the effort or that it will benefit them directly or indirectly. The systematic discrediting of the rescue archaeological research of building sites and of finds which originate from them has resulted from the theoretical framework of archaeological excavation since the beginning of the 20th century up to the present day. Moreover, when a rescue excavation is carried out, there is an old-fashioned perception of its documentation which excludes any information which does not serve the antiquarian aspect of the investigation, but which can reveal relationships between the site and the contemporary urban fabric and building regulations (Raftopoulou, 1998; van Leusen et al 2009). Consequently, the few building sites which are actually excavated are not treated as discreet archaeological sites, so the opportunity to examine the spatial relationships between the individual archaeological plots themselves and with non-archaeological plots which have also been uncovered is lost. In addition, the post-excavation analysis and the dissemination of the archaeological information which derives from this take place at a very slow pace, which makes it difficult for an interested party to benefit from documented information quickly enough (Kraut, 2007: 49; Koukouli Chrysanthaki, 2007: 94; Gleeson, 2007: 144; Djurič, 2007: 185; Schauman Lönnqvist, 2007: 53).

As a consequence, the citizens who experience this situation are not proud of antiquities which are found on their land, nor do they perceive them as important, even if they are generally proud of the history of the place where they live (Herzfeld, 2003[1991]: 364). Their relationship with the archaeological remains of their area is influenced to a great extent by their perception of the existing archaeological sites in the city and the historical centre. In many cases, those responsible are unable to maintain the designated archaeological sites in a good condition and accessible to the public (Zois, 1990: 59; Papakonstantinou,

2003: 23, 26; Varvitsiotis, 2005; Papageorgiou-Venetas, 1994: 323). Moreover, a common complaint on the part of the inhabitants of many cities in many countries is that historical centres, even after their revitalisation, become problematic as a result of changes to their demographic structure due to economic dependence on tourism, and because the monuments remain unconnected with the existing urban fabric and functions such as transportation (Sarantakou, 2000: 314; Orbasli, 2000; Pickard, 2001). At the same time, there are a number of examples from modern everyday life, where the management of important archaeological remains which are discovered on private land, public land or in the streets of a city becomes the object of political pressure, vote soliciting and speculation (Philippides, 2005: 54-55).

A shift in this negative attitude may come from the addition of the concept 'sustainability' to the development agenda. By the term 'sustainable development' is meant the rational management of natural resources so that contemporary generations can meet their needs, but at the same time save resources to meet the needs of future generations (Chatzimbiros, 1997: 477; Evans, 1997:6). This model presupposes the sensible management not only of natural but also of cultural heritage, since people are seen as beings with both physical and social needs, and as deserving a thorough examination of their distinctive characteristics (Collective Volume, 2001: 15-16). As far as archaeological research and city planning are concerned, there is no framework for adopting sustainable practices, such as discouraging construction companies from starting projects on archaeological sites, known or potential, and preventing rescue excavations when they can be avoided (Koukouli Chrysanthaki, 2004: 477; Kakouris, 2004b: 500; Triantafyllos, 2004: 187; Bozoki Ernyey, 2007b: 12; Schauman Lönnqvist, 2007: 53; Koukouli Chrysanthaki, 2007: 94; Gleeson, 2007: 144).

To this end, the constantly developing field of information technology could play a role, even though, as was demonstrated in the previous chapter, its use is limited as far as the management of the underlying cultural heritage of a city is concerned (Zinglersen, 2004: 147). In numerous cities around the world, including many in Greece, there are no organised or updated databases (Doerr & Iorizzo, 2008). Therefore, the opportunity is lost for interested parties to process all kinds of information about the city, as well as the chance to test the quality of that information and to standardise it (Schlader, 2002: 518; Palumbo, 1993: 184; Mehrer, 2002; Wheatley & Gillings, 2002: 83; Semeraro, 1993: 206).

The adoption of GIS technology in particular would allow a different approach to urban archaeological phenomena, with an emphasis on their spatial analysis, the testing of the statistical significance of observations and the generation of new information (Wheatley & Gillings, 2002; Kvamme, 1999; Conolly & Lake, 2006). Besides, this technology can ensure the more complete implementation of legal reforms and commitments which stem from national legislation and the country's participation in international fora.

3.2 Management of the underlying archaeological resources in the city: Questions and tools

As has been seen, it is clear that it is necessary to treat archaeological research as part of the procedure of city planning and construction. The simultaneous development of the methodologies of the related disciplines, with the aim of achieving harmonious cooperation within the statutory stages of planning, may improve the relationship between the inhabitants and their city, its present and its past.

As a contribution to the formulation of a model of cooperation and management of city planning activity and archaeological research the following basic questions are addressed:

1. Is it feasible to use basic archaeological information to predict the potential existence of antiquities which we are not aware of?
2. How can the prediction be evaluated quantitatively and qualitatively in order to determine its reliability?
3. If archaeological and existing city planning information are combined, can the conclusions that are drawn be incorporated into the city planning procedure and enrich it in such a way as to serve the needs of the citizens and to fulfil the obligations of the state?

In order to answer these questions which arise the 'innovative' use of tried and tested methods is proposed, such as the methodology of landscape archaeology in archaeological research and cultural management within the city plan, the use of available sources of information which to date have not been the subject of study, that is, of excavations (both archaeological and non-archaeological), and, finally, the use of interdisciplinary applications within existing institutional frameworks.

3.2.1 New uses for known methods (landscape archaeology)

The Mediterranean basin constituted one of the first fields where the research methodology of landscape archaeology was developed. Particularly in Greece, since the 1950s until the present day, numerous small, intensive surface surveys have been carried out. Thus, considerable experience has accumulated and been published (Farinetti, 2011; Bevan & Conolly, 2009; Hatzinikolaou et al 2003; Wiseman & Zachos, 2003; Simoni & Papagiannopoulos, 1998; Bintliff et al 2007).

The Greek countryside is characterised by a continuous distribution of artefacts of archaeological significance. This observation has led to the formulation of the concept of the archaeological site within the study area, depending on the density of the distribution of the finds on the ground. Thus, the study area is divided into sites, peripheries of sites, and non-sites, depending on the scope of each survey. Each

site takes on properties and characteristics which can be both analysed quantitatively and georeferenced. Since the first expeditions were organised by foreign archaeological schools, their questions and objectives were purely investigative and antiquarian and they were not interested, at least to begin with, in the concept of management.

The proposed approach is in correspondence with this practice, but in contrast with standard practice of urban archaeology, in which the whole city is treated as a unified site. As a landscape can be read all the space which is occupied by a modern city and as sites or non-sites can be read the positions of excavations where antiquities have or have not been found, respectively. Every point corresponds to an entry in the database and is accompanied by its georeference and a series of other characteristics, variables or parameters. As, more importantly, the database allows it, the objective is more the management of cultural heritage, without neglecting the antiquarian dimension and the identification of relationships and potential archaeological patterns.

Conducting investigations at the level of the city reduces the risk of giving in to environmental determinism and leads instead to being more open to anthropogenic parameters. Furthermore, in contemporary cities the construction sector affects the prevailing environmental conditions. As a result, a large part of the environmental and palaeoenvironmental material exists in disturbed layers or has even disappeared. Moreover, environmental diversity, which is visible at national and regional levels, is rendered invisible at the local level, like that of a medium-sized city (Allen, 2000:102). The same message seems to be put across by the City Plan, which does not distinguish the environmental factors and, therefore, the background is a morphologically isotropic environment from an administrative perspective, consisting of buildable land and communal land, on both of which certain building and land use regulations apply.

The recording of all excavated sites, whether they have antiquities or not, is not a widespread practice in urban archaeology, even though it constitutes written documentation of knowledge which has been passed on orally to date, and is based on the experience of archaeologists, wardens, etc. The non-existence of archaeological traces in the earth is just as significant information as the knowledge of the existence of antiquities, because it enables the documentation of the boundaries not only of known but also of new archaeological sites which are dotted around the urban fabric of the contemporary city. Given that the majority of archaeological excavations within a city are of the rescue type, and are restricted to plots which are being built on, it may be necessary for some time to pass, maybe even decades, until the continuation of the site on neighbouring plots is excavated. Only after that does the gradual detection or not of antiquities on adjacent properties complete the puzzle of the ancient city.

The faith which landscape archaeologists have had in quantitative analysis, statistical manipulation and spatial analysis has not been mirrored in urban archaeology. In the latter a stubborn insistence on the classic method of rescue excavation is evident, with all the problems which that entails. However, modern technology and digital applications can be adopted in the full knowledge of their capabilities and limitations and always bearing in mind the need for the constant testing and confirmation of the method and any conclusions drawn.

Finally, the practical advantages of landscape archaeology studies are that they are economical and less demanding in terms of bureaucracy and obtaining permits. Conversely, major disadvantages of archaeological research in cities are the burden of its high cost and bureaucratic inflexibility which both private investors and the state are obliged to shoulder.

3.2.2 Ground disturbance as a source of information

Excavation is every kind of work which requires ground disturbance and the removal of earth. Rescue excavation refers to the systematic and methodological removal of layers of earth in order to locate and record archaeological finds prior to the commencement of construction work on a building site (Renfrew & Bahn, 1991: 90-93) and usually follows an excavation, if antiquities are discovered. Thus it can be seen that they are two distinct concepts. In contrast to a rescue excavation, an excavation constitutes an available but, to date, insufficiently exploited source of information which, however, could be made use of. Excavations are not usually recorded or studied scientifically in the same way as rescue excavations. Furthermore, they do not discriminate between sites with or those without archaeological potential. In this way, though, they offer a valuable source of information, since the aim of archaeological research is not only to locate antiquities where they are expected to be, but also where there was thought to be little chance of any existing (Dore & Wandsnider, 2006). This advantage is ensured by studying all the excavations, because then there is no other criterion for sampling but the excavation itself.

Since excavations have proved to be a basic source of information, the establishment of a system of monitoring them and drawing up reports by the Archaeological Service is to be encouraged. The administrative measures which must be taken in order to implement this proposal are incorporated into the wider spirit and letter of existing legislation and do not presuppose reforms or changes to the law. Nor does this solution presuppose the development of procedures which require years to be integrated into the existing system or the creation of new scientific or administrative organisations. There are measures which could be taken immediately and would have an effect in the short and medium term. They are based on the functioning and activation of the existing organisation of the Archaeological Service for the management of construction works in which antiquities are discovered.

The most important archaeological information which the representative of the Service is called on to record, once antiquities have been discovered at an excavation, is just that, in other words, the existence of ancient remains and the interruption of the work. This information is neither contrary to nor contravenes the exclusive right of the archaeologists/excavators to publish the results of their investigation in the future as stipulated by Law 3028, 2002: Article 39. From these entries a database can be created quickly and comparatively easily. It can be based on the completion of a simple form, which stands for an excavation report. This report is completed on the spot during the excavation by the representative. The form requires care but not particularly specialised knowledge, so that it can be completed by a warden if an archaeologist is not present.

In addition, the updating of the resultant database can take place immediately, since it does not require specialised information, initially at least, but is related to the details which are submitted for planning permission to be issued. The geocoding of the database and its incorporation into a GIS opens the way for new forms of data manipulation as digital cartographic layers, suitable for statistical and spatial analysis. Each entry in the database, which arises from the digitisation of information from excavation reports, continues to be added later, each time with new variables, which arise either during the rescue excavation work or after it has been finished. The updating is gradual and always takes into account the progress of the investigation and new knowledge, while the models which are constructed are subject to repeated evaluation.

To serve the needs of this book, the term 'non-archaeological' excavation is introduced in contrast to the term 'archaeological excavation'. The latter refers to a case where antiquities are discovered due to ground disturbance during an excavation. By contrast, the former defines every excavation during which antiquities are not discovered, so it is not subsequently necessary to conduct a rescue excavation.

3.2.3 Interdisciplinary collaboration and opening up to society

The main aim of studies in urban archaeology is usually to locate traces of ancient habitation in contemporary cities and to interpret them. There are no studies which clearly connect the ancient palimpsest with the modern city and current city planning information, such as building regulations. Wherever such studies were conducted, their basic weakness proved to be the fact that archaeological research and the drawing of purely archaeological conclusions came first, and were subsequently simply handed over to the Local Planning Authority. However, the starting point for the studies could be the work of the Local Planning Authority and particularly the procedure for granting planning permission in order to investigate archaeological data.

The aim of the present study and its subsequent proposal is to connect the archaeological procedure with the city planning reality and then cultural heritage management, within the framework of city planning. In addition, whereas publications to date concern known antiquities which have been discovered in cities and historical centres as well as monuments still standing, the focus of this approach is mainly unknown antiquities which will be discovered, that is, whose existence is conjectured.

According to this approach, information will be managed in such a way as to be comprehensible and useful, not only for archaeologists, but also for engineers, contractors, investors, landowners, etc., in the form of lists, explanatory texts and maps which will be at their disposal. Each entry constitutes a locality in the City Plan area and consequently may be connected with a host of other variables apart from archaeological ones, related to all kinds of regional, developmental, environmental and city planning.

Besides, interdisciplinary communication and cooperation is provided for, both by national legislation and international conventions (Council of Europe, 1992), and wherever it has been implemented, it has proved to be a challenge but also the key to satisfying all the interested parties (Willems, 2008; Dalla Bona, 2000). This enables this specific proposal to apply generally, assuming that the following prerequisites are met: a) the foundations of a construction project require ground disturbance and b) private individuals and the institutional bodies involved are inspired by faith in the value of protecting archaeological heritage and conform to the relevant national legislation.

The ultimate achievement of the implementation of the proposal, both concerning cultural heritage management and interdisciplinary communication, will be not only the construction of predictive models of potential archaeological layers in a city, but also the adaptation of building regulations to the possibility of finding antiquities at an excavation.

In the case of predictive models, all interested parties are informed of the possibility of their works encountering antiquities on their property in the planning phase before the work begins. This information can be made use of by landowners or by potential purchasers who, among other criteria for choosing where to invest, can include the chances of there being antiquities in the ground where they are interested in laying foundations. As far as building regulations are concerned, it is possible for some to be adopted with the criterion of the potential existence of antiquities in certain areas and at certain depths.

3.3 Expected outcomes

The anticipated results of such an approach can be summarised as the following:

The citizens are at the centre of a comprehensive plan for the space where they live and work, so that their personal and family development is not hindered, and their construction plans are regulated in such a way that they do not suffer any losses without wishing to or expecting to.

The inhabitants and users of a city are reconciled with their cultural environment and the subjective value which they attach to the space at any given moment is enhanced (Fairclough, 2003: 310). The citizens' interest in history and art is renewed, and their need for respect for and maintenance of their cultural identity is satisfied.

The historical complexity of the contemporary city is highlighted and the role of planning is redefined by the simple technical process of drawing up plans, in a comprehensive procedure of intervention and decision-making (Christophilopoulos, 2002:41).

The source of tension which usually characterises relationships between archaeologists, city planners, building contractors, landowners, individuals and institutional bodies of the state or local authorities is reduced and/or eradicated. Furthermore, a bank of archaeological data is constructed, 'translated' into a language comprehensible to city planners and to the centres of decision making. Each one asserts their role within the existing institutional environment without submitting to pressure.

The full implementation of legislation is accelerated, concerning the protection of antiquities (Law 3028, 2002), planning (Law 2508, 1997) and sustainable development (Law 2742, 1999).

A body of information which can clarify the archaeological physiognomy of a city is utilised to the full, by combining the findings of archaeological research which has been carried out in the city for many decades with modern technology, specifically, that of GIS and Spatial Analysis. Moreover, weaknesses are identified in the implementation of research in the city and in relation to building regulations, and ways of removing those weaknesses are proposed.

3.4 Conclusion

Thus far reference has been made to the theoretical framework which surrounds the management of the underground cultural heritage of a city. Furthermore, the research questions have been posed and the expected benefits of the development of a pioneering method of managing archaeological information in city planning have been stated.

In the chapters which follow specific applications for processing and dealing with the themes which have so far been approached theoretically will be presented. The main focus of the applications is construction activity in Patras during the five-year period 2004-2008. For that reason, first the archaeological physiognomy of the city will be presented, as well as its urban development since the establishment of the Greek state.

Chapter 4

Model Construction

4.1 Methodology

The theoretical framework concerning the management of cultural heritage and that of archaeological remains below a contemporary city in combination with the methodological tools provided by technology, particularly GIS, leads us to the development of an application which will answer the crucial questions which were formulated in the previous chapters.

Initially, this could be achieved by determining potential archaeological sites in areas of the city which, though as yet unexcavated, appear promising due to their proximity to known and excavated ancient sites, making use of information derived from the hundreds of excavations which take place in a city every year. At a more advanced stage of the investigation the identification of potential archaeological and non-archaeological sites is insufficient. Therefore, the potential depth of archaeological layers at those sites is also sought. This information, once incorporated into a city database, can act as a catalyst for the adaptation of the parameters being studied in city planning, and even for the introduction of new building regulations.

The success of such an endeavour depends on the extent to which the procedures that are anticipated at each stage are tested quantitatively and qualitatively, in order to ensure their reliability and to encourage the spirit of cooperation between partners who, at first sight, appear to have conflicting objectives and interests, such as the Archaeological Service and the Local Planning Authority.

At the centre of this application, however, remain the citizens, individually and collectively, since it is their recognised right to develop personal initiatives on the one hand, and to preserve their cultural identity and heritage on the other, as well as to enjoy sustainable conditions in their city.

For the case study the city of Patras was selected, and specifically the area included in the approved City Plan. The case study presupposes a detailed knowledge of archaeological and city planning data of the chosen area as well as available accumulated experience. The knowledge is derived from research into the bibliography and archives. The experience is recorded by means of structured interviews using a common questionnaire with practitioners who are or have been involved in the recent past in city planning and/or the management of underground cultural heritage in the selected area. The review of the literature provides information related to the archaeological and historical background of the city, such as what has been discovered by archaeological, and principally, rescue archaeological studies in the city and the testimony of historical sources. Since the review of the archives covers the recent past too, material concerning the evolution of the city originates from plans that were and continue to be drawn up from 1828 to the present day. As far as the quantitative analysis is concerned, the data comes from excavations which took place within the approved City Plan of Patras during the period 2004-2008 on plots of land, public spaces and the road network of the city included in the archives of the 6th Directorate of Prehistoric and Classical Antiquities, i.e. the local office of the Archaeological Service.

An excavation, that is, a ground disturbance and the removal of a quantity of earth, is the first sine qua non stage of the work and the foundation of a construction project, be it below or above ground level. At this stage antiquities will either be found or not and the archaeological information will be recorded in a rudimentary fashion with at least a YES or a NO. The data is digitally processed and analysed, spatially and statistically, so that the hidden dimension of the information is highlighted and new data is produced. This is the nature of predictive models when GIS technology is adopted. Furthermore, by means of a series of tests archaeological data and city planning regulations are correlated and the behaviour of individual variables when they correlate is studied, as is how these affect the final form of the city and its cultural heritage management.

Despite the fact that it is not referred to separately, an important factor in the development and application of such an approach, but also in the formulation of any position, is the quality of the data and the accuracy with which it has been recorded at the different stages of its manipulation. Consequently, at every step the procedures which are followed are subject to constant testing and evaluation. The evaluation is carried out either by means of quantitative methods offered by a GIS or using qualitative data, such as the findings of old rescue excavations in the city which took place and were published before the period being examined here.

For this reason the connection between the stages is not strictly linear. Each stage interacts with more than one other stage and the aim of constructing the best model and drawing the most accurate conclusions is never completed, since new research will always yield new data to be processed.

4.2 Patras as a case study

The City Plan of Patras was selected as the study area (Fig. 4.1), because it is a city with a history stretching back many centuries, with well-documented rescue excavations (Sklavenitis & Staikos, 2005), and which still hides archaeological secrets within its subsoil. Hundreds of archaeological sites have been found over the years. The majority of the rescue excavations have not been published completely. However, a number of articles have succeeded in reconstructing parts of the palimpsest lying beneath the contemporary city (Fig. 4.2).

Archaeological evidence of habitation dates as far back as the Early Bronze Age (c. 2500 B.C.) (Stavropoulou Gatsi, 2001). Archaeological research throughout the city has also revealed prehistoric settlements and burial sites (Papazoglou Manioudaki, 1993) of the Middle and Late Bronze Age.

The archaeological evidence is relatively poor as regards the centuries that follow with only a few burial sites of the Geometric era (Stavropoulou Gatsi et al 2006: 84) and scattered remains of the Archaic period. The Classical and Hellenistic periods (5th c. onwards) are better represented

Fig. 4.1: The distribution of buildings within the boundaries of the City Plan according to the 2001 survey (Source: Laboratory of Urban and Regional Planning – University of Patras).

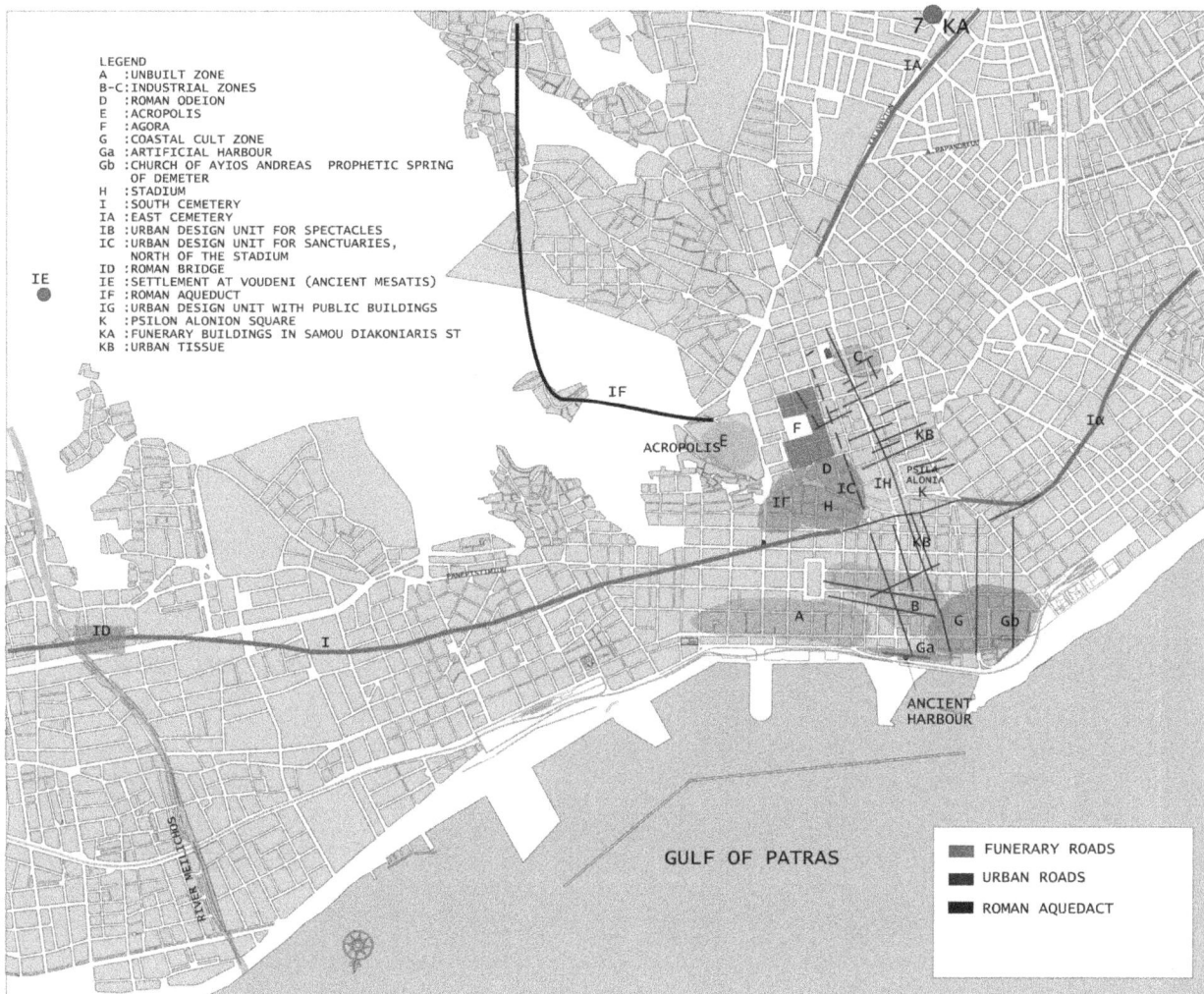

Fig. 4.2: The city plan of ancient Patras (Source: Rizakis & Petropoulos, 2005: 32-33, Courtesy of Staikos Editions).

with remains of the city wall, streets, burial sites and a road network that has dictated the main road axes ever since. As the city entered the Roman era (146 B.C.), it experienced a new stage of development. The city expanded to the sea and a colony for veterans of the naval battle of Actium was founded by Augustus in 14 B.C. A dense road network from the Roman era has been discovered as well as a great number of public and private buildings of rural and urban types, workshops, cemeteries, the harbour, etc. The city flourished until the end of the 3rd c. A.D. when population degradation and impoverishment is recorded in literary sources. Building activity resumed from 4th to 6th c., when the main infrastructure and buildings underwent renovation. A new demographic decline took place between 7th and 9th c. followed by a new period of development in economic, social and intellectual life that is evident in archaeological research. During the period 1446-1828 Patras was part of the Ottoman Empire, with the exception of a thirty-year-long occupation by the Venetians (1687-1715). Several travellers and writers describe a settlement with small poor houses, churches, a mosque and a central market (Georgopoulou Verra, 1997; Vingopoulou, 2005) built round the Castle, a fortification dating to the 6th c. A.D., which succeeded a Prehistoric and Classical acropolis at the same location.

Contemporary Patras is more or less the result of an ongoing building and planning process that started in 1828, after liberation from the Ottoman occupation and the establishment of the Greek state. The first plan of modern Patras was designed by the military engineer Stamatios Voulgaris in 1829 (Fig. 4.3).

By dividing Patras into upper and lower parts, he respected an ancient spatial organization, which allowed different functions of the city to evolve. The original plan designated a no-build zone between the two sections. The zone contained the Castle as well as monuments dating from the Classical to the Ottoman era. Had it been realized, it would have constituted one of the first archaeological parks of the 19th c. In this way, the original plan managed to combine the protection of archaeological heritage with the important role of the green zone not only from an aesthetic point of view, but also as a factor that enhances people's well-being, sanitation and the climate.

The plan was never fully realized and several others followed, each one adding more buildable space. The post-war sociopolitical development in Greece allowed the emergence of certain characteristics that shaped the pathology of the Greek urban planning system in the

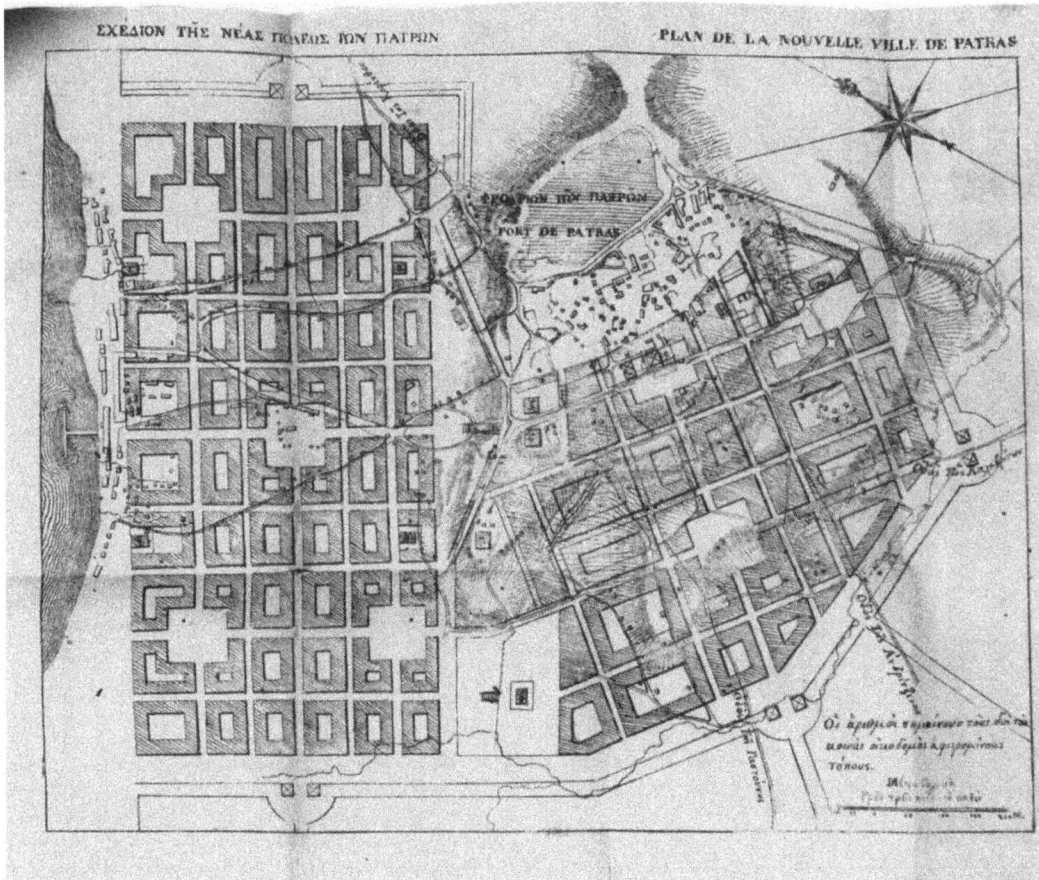

Fig. 4.3: The Voulgaris Plan of Patras (Source: Kardamitsi Adami, 1996: 198).

second half of the 20th c., such as unauthorized expansion, illegal construction, a lack of efficient control mechanisms and insufficient mapping of private and public land (Oikonomou, 2000: 44). Since 1829 the city has expanded in all possible directions (Papadatou Giannopoulou, 1991: 42), engulfing rural land and privatising public space.

Moreover, the modern face of the city is constantly changing, since it is continuously evolving in terms of its economy and construction (Polydorides et al 1985: 23-24; Pappas, 2006). Characteristic examples of these changes which happened during the period of the case study are the completion of the Rio-Antirrio Bridge, which gave a boost to construction activity and the development of new infrastructure in the wider area, works for the so-called 'inner' bypass and the Diakoniaris river, as well as smaller scale public and private works. As these works took place both within and outside the centre of the city, they offered the opportunity for widespread archaeological research, which was particularly enlightening as far as the urban and peri-urban archaeology of the city is concerned.

Unluckily, the unbuildable archaeological zone of the original plan gradually shrank, monuments disappeared and private housing emerged in the area. Yet the task of the local Archaeological Service was only recently facilitated by the implementation of the new archaeological law, which demands that protection of monuments and archaeological sites be taken into account at all levels of planning and development schemes (Law 3028, 2002: Article 3). Thus, there is enough material to connect the Patras of yesterday and today with the Patras of tomorrow.

The Patras of tomorrow emerges through the most recent city planning proposals which have been formulated and submitted. The Regulatory (Master) Plan of Patras and the General Urban Plan of the Municipality of Patras constitute different tools for the implementation of the National Territorial Plan, the Regional Territorial Plan for the Region of Western Greece and the aims of the Prefecture of Achaia (Theorema, 2007: 2; Pantazis et al 2006: 1). With these proposals Law 2508/1997 was implemented. The Regulatory Plan defines the developmental objectives of the wider metropolitan area of Patras and the actions necessary to achieve them (Theorema, 2009). The General Urban Plan defines the objectives for the spatial and city planning of the Municipality of Patras (Pantazis et al 2006: 1).

Focusing on those points of the plans which concern cultural heritage management, it can be ascertained that archaeological remains which gradually come to light during excavational work are poorly dealt with. Despite the obvious cultural wealth of the city, the guidelines do not seem to have been influenced at all by that fact and not to have taken it into account, except in a few very special cases, although it is admitted that it represents one of the comparative advantages of the area.

Moreover, in the City Plan, which determines the building regulations, the public spaces and the permitted land uses (Christophilopoulos, 1997: 102), the archaeological background is not fully recognised (Simoni, 2014). Apart from certain archaeological sites and monuments it is not included in the public spaces. It depicts principally ecclesiastical monuments and their grounds. There are just three purely archaeological sites: the prehistoric settlement of Pagona, the Roman aqueduct and the Roman bridge, as well as the Roman odeum, which, although constituting part of a wider archaeological area with many expropriated plots of land, do not appear anywhere as such. The remaining seven designated archaeological sites and monuments within the City Plan are located on street blocks, most of which are subject to building regulations and permitted land uses.

Furthermore, another 34 excavated house plots, most of which have been purchased by the state because they contain antiquities that must be preserved, are completely ignored, as if they have no role to play in the planning of the city.

This weakness reflects the entire city planning process. The city plan of Patras is not in tune with the commitment to protect and safeguard as yet unexplored cultural heritage which is known to be hidden under the surface. It is therefore necessary to examine in particular the connection between the archaeological resources of the city and city planning, and to propose changes which would tie in with the idea of a comprehensive plan from the point of view of managing underground cultural heritage. This is the aim of the applications which follow.

It should be noted that unlike other Greek cities there are excavation reports in Patras, which come from the construction projects in the city. They are what constitute the primary material to be used in this book. Besides, the archaeological material which was used for the research of this book, and the archaeological investigations which have yielded this material have not been published before and were only available to the author after permission was granted by the Local Board of Antiquities.

Furthermore, the rich archaeological knowledge that has been accumulated for the city by the Archaeological Service has yielded a map (Fig. 4.2). This will be useful for testing the digital models that will be presented in this book.

4.2.1 Interviewing the experts

Before proceeding to the quantitative analysis, it is worthwhile examining the way in which the two main fields of science which are involved in cultural heritage management, those of the archaeologists and the planners, interact through city planning. Their multifaceted characteristics will be presented, and how updated they are regarding topics which concern the 'opposing' field will be determined. This is achieved by means of interviews with

related scientists and practitioners in Patras with a common questionnaire.

The interviews took place in November 2011. The answers which were given are typical of interviews with 'specialists'. In other words, they exhibit a creative familiarity with the questions at hand, because they are about topics that concern specialists on a regular basis (Chorianopoulos, 2006: 167) and due to which they have acquired a satisfactory level of information, they have developed particular behaviour and can invoke a wealth of examples in order to support their positions. Even the more technical questions gave the interviewees the opportunity to raise issues regarding scientific ethics, public concern and government policy.

Table 4.1: The questionnaire

- How do you judge the provisions of the existing institutional framework for cooperation between the local Directorates of the Ministry of Culture and the City Planning department in matters concerning (city) planning and the development of the city of Patras?

- Should the Planning departments of municipal and regional authorities, and/or private planners be staffed with archaeologists and vice versa (the Archaeological Service with city planners) who will have a planning/ decision-making role at a local level, which will not be based on a linear planning rationale?

- To what extent does the existing planning procedure recognise archaeological research and incorporate it into the planning of the city at any level (Master Plan, General Urban Plan and City Plan)?

- Do you consider that the archaeological sites and expropriated land are adequately depicted in the City Plan of Patras and to what extent do the existing recorded spaces represent an obstacle to development and city planning?

- Is the possibility of constructing of a building project over antiquities taken into consideration so that its location can be adjusted to avoid that happening?

- Do the legal owners of any construction project (private individuals or public bodies) have a right to know beforehand the chances of their project being constructed over antiquities?

- Would it be useful for the legal owners of projects (private individuals or public bodies) to know where their land coincides with a potential archaeological site and at what depth the archaeological layer is estimated to be, so that they can act accordingly (shallower foundations, etc.)?

- Do you believe that the adoption of quantitative methods, statistical tests and computer applications (e.g. Spatial Analysis, GIS) in urban archaeology would contribute to city planning and the developmental prospects of the city?

- Have you ever used such methods?

- Do you have anything else to add?

The full transcript of the interviews and the list of interviewees have been published in the appendices of my doctoral thesis and are available at http://hdl.handle. net/10889/7294. From the answers which were given it became obvious that an effort is being made to practise each profession within the existing framework, an effort that is characterised by an understanding for the 'other', insomuch as that is allowed or imposed by that framework. The interviewees admitted that cooperation regarding matters of city planning, cultural heritage management and the development of the city is difficult to achieve on an everyday basis, due to various complications of the procedure itself, even though cooperation and the exchange of information are essential ingredients for the successful performance of the planning and decision-making role which some have in the planning of the city. Generally, it was accepted that laws exist, but that their enforcement is the result of efforts which sometimes lead to the preservation of monuments, while other times it leads to their destruction, despite the feasibility of less extreme solutions.

Almost everyone agreed that the use of archaeological knowledge is useful to predict the location of potential archaeological sites, in order for them to be avoided during construction work and for the destruction of ancient layers to be prevented. In particular, the developer of a construction project, whether a private individual or a public body, 'ought', 'has a right' or 'is obliged' to be aware of the possibility of discovering archaeological layers as far down as the foundations or even deeper.

On the contrary, the idea of changing the depth of foundations in order to avoid potential archaeological layers did not meet with agreement from the majority, who believed that in this way the investigation would be interrupted. Moreover, they connected the progress of research directly with the speedy payment of compensation to the affected party for the extra expenses incurred by the inevitable delay. However, they all recognise that the timely payment of compensation will become all the more difficult in the current economic situation.

Concerning the use of new technologies for the application of various quantitative methods and analyses, the interviewees agreed that it is now difficult to avoid the use of computers. This is because, especially regarding city planning and the developmental prospects of a city, digital applications contribute to a more accurate picture of the existing situation and the planning proposal as a whole, and not only of data of a cultural content.

A question was posed specifically regarding the recording of archaeological sites and plots of land expropriated by the Ministry of Culture. The answers given demonstrated there was confusion as to how much of the data in the possession of the Archaeological Service is made available to planners and local authorities, and what data researchers and local authorities ask for to formulate plans at the multiple steps of planning. It seems that the exchange of basic information between public services and planners is not to be taken for

granted, perhaps because it is not clearly determined what everyone involved needs to know.

They all agreed, though, that not only do the existing and recorded cultural sites not constitute an obstacle to development, but, on the contrary, that they enrich city planning. They actually serve as an opportunity for the creation of attractions in the city and a challenge for yet more creative planning solutions.

4.3 The data

The Archaeological Service of Patras has been entrusted to date with the responsibility for granting planning permission and the investigation of excavations in the Patras area. The staff monitor excavations and inform their supervisors if antiquities are found. Despite the fact that this procedure has been followed by the Archaeological Service since 1985, during the first 15 years of its implementation the supervisory authority was only informed orally by the employees who inspected the excavations. For reasons related to the functional environment of the Archaeological Service and the overcoming of bureaucratic inflexibility, only during the last decade and only in Patras and the surrounding area has a written report been submitted, a form on which the employees fill in the relevant fields as well as their observations.

In this way, plots of land which have no antiquities are also recorded, information which is just as important as the knowledge of the existence of antiquities. Furthermore, the depth to which the excavator digs is recorded, along with some first observations about the composition of the soil.

4.3.1 Data collecting - Limitations

Recognising the importance of excavation reports for the management of archaeological information and by extension the management of cultural heritage in the city, the reports of the period 2004-2008 were examined.

A supplementary source was the records of rescue excavations at the Archaeological Service. These records contain all the rescue excavations which have been carried out by the Archaeological Service from 1983 up to the present day. Wherever feasible, the rescue excavation diaries were examined, as well as other files containing applications and decisions. Finally, further information was then gathered from discussions with service employees themselves: archaeologists, wardens, technicians and clerks. Using these sources, the material which constitutes the database was gathered.

For every site, whether it had antiquities or not, the maximum known depth without antiquities was examined. For the non-archaeological excavations, this value is equal to the intended excavation depth, which usually coincides with the depth of the foundations of the work. This information is derived from the excavation report. For the archaeological excavations, this figure is equal to the minimum depth of discovery of architectural remains or other archaeological finds during the rescue excavation. The information concerning the maximum known depth without antiquities provides a limit within the soil, down to which there are no visible signs of past use.

The database also includes city planning regulations which characterise the buildings in each part of the city, the most important being the floor area ratio (f.a.r.). This is '*the number which, if multiplied by the surface area of a building plot, gives the total surface area of the floors of buildings which are permitted to be constructed on that building plot*' (Law 1577, 1985: Article 2.27). It is the basic parameter for the exploitation of a plot of land (Christophilopoulos, 1988: 43).

The form of the building under construction and the size of the project are both based on two further regulations, maximum permitted height (m.p.h.) and maximum permitted coverage (m.p.c). The m.p.h. is defined as the '*height of the highest level of the building, above which all construction is forbidden, except for facilities which are permitted in special cases and in a limited fashion*', (Law 1577, 1985: Article 2.31). The m.p.c. of a building plot is defined as '*the sum of the maximum area which is allowed to be covered by the total area of the plot of land*' (Law 1577, 1985: Article 2.26).

Building regulations apply only to building plots and consequently those excavations which take place on street blocks. By extension, all the other excavations take place in unbuildable public space, that is, '*all kinds of roads, squares, parkland and generally open spaces designated for public use, which are determined by the approved street plan of the settlement or have been set aside for public use in any other legal manner*' (Law 1577, 1985: Article 2.2).

A further piece of information which was recorded for the research was the defrayment of the expenses of a rescue excavation by private individuals, the landowners. Frequently, owners of plots of land on which antiquities are discovered and there is going to be a rescue excavation prefer to defray the cost of conducting the rescue excavation themselves, if at that time the Archaeological Service does not have its own team available due to a heavy workload, lack of staff, etc. In this case the rescue excavation is supervised by the Archaeological Service, but the owner is charged for the remuneration of the staff, the purchase of equipment and whatever other costs are incurred. However, the process of returning the plot to its owner is speeded up, something which many owners consider worth the extra expense.

In terms of the duration of the rescue excavation, as well as the time which elapses from one phase to the next (start of rescue excavation, end of rescue excavation, determination of preservation status, etc.), the obstacle of irregular recording was faced. Although for many cases it was possible to find and crosscheck data, there were a number of cases where the data was minimal and fragmentary.

Finally, wherever rescue excavations were conducted, further data was recorded related to the finds (chronology, typology) and their preservation status (reburial, demolition, removal).

4.3.2 Data digitisation

Every excavation of a building plot was digitised as a point which was placed wherever possible in the centre of its surface. The digitisation of the road network was carried out in the form of points. For all the excavations for which the point was recorded with the accuracy of a street number, e.g., '*Lontou Street, in front of number 22-24*', the digitisation was carried out as single points. For the rest, because they were referred to linearly in the report, e.g., '*Agiou Dimitriou Street, from Pantokratoras Street to Germanou Street*', more points were used along the axis of the excavation, which were naturally numbered differently (Fig. 4.4).

The digital cartographic background which was used for the points of the excavations was from the Hellenic Statistical Authority and had been constructed in 2001 for the needs of a population census and a building survey. The reference system is the Hellenic Geodetic Reference System 1987 (EGSA 87). The recently updated digital map of the approved City Plan of Patras was also used.

4.3.3 Tools of Spatial Analysis

At this point the most important techniques of spatial analysis that were applied in the present project will be presented and the properties which render them necessary for the manipulation of the spatial data of a city will be underlined.

Spatial Autocorrelation

Spatial autocorrelation is a property which describes the proximity or not of similar values of a variable in a space. Positive autocorrelation is the name given to the situation where similar values of a variable form clusters, whereas negative autocorrelation refers to the property of similar values lying at a distance from each other (Wheatley and Gillings, 2002: 131). The Global Moran's and Getis-Ord General tests are two tools for examining spatial autocorrelation. They each calculate one value, I and G respectively, the z-score and the probability p-value on a specified level of statistical significance α. In each case, if p>α, then the distribution of the data is random. In the opposite case, the statistically significant data indicates some kind of spatial autocorrelation. The Global Moran's test demonstrates whether the autocorrelation is positive or negative. The Getis-Ord General test shows whether there is positive autocorrelation of the high or low values of the variable (Fletcher, 2008: 2049; Anselin, 1993b: 4,6).

Since, however, spatial information can consist of a few tens to many thousands of entries, the higher the number of entries, the more inadequate the general tests of this

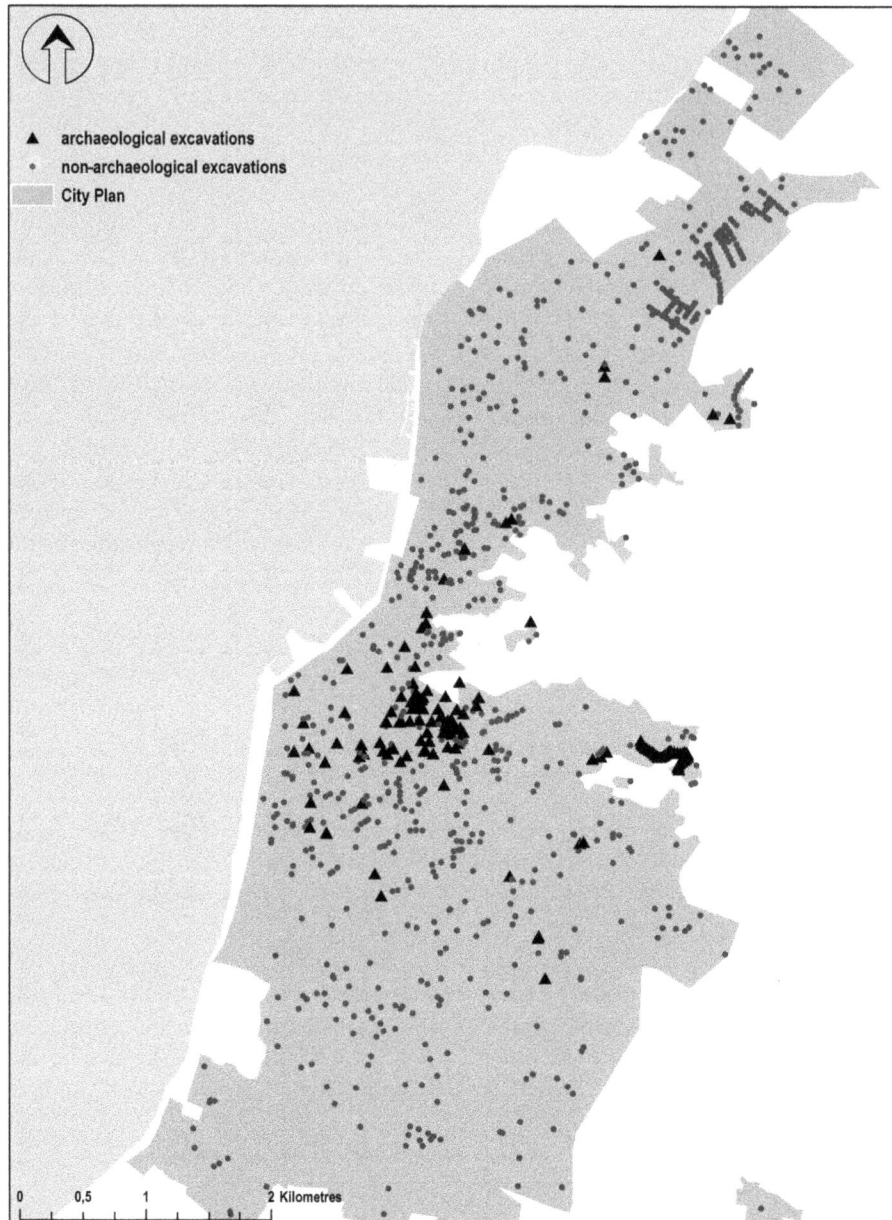

Fig. 4.4: The distribution of the data within the City Plan of Patras.

type become, because they cannot describe the various local patterns of distribution which are concealed within the general picture of the information (Anselin, 1993a:3). This need is met by the test at a local level and facilitates the analysis of the data locally. Although the general test is more widespread, only the local test can detect the local statistically significant outliers and clusters. Anselin Local Moran's I is such a test (Premo, 2004: 856-857; Anselin, 1993a). The test is used to explore to what extent the points of the archaeological excavations and the points of the non-archaeological excavations present some kind of autocorrelation and where exactly this lies in the area of study.

Thiessen Polygons

Thiessen polygons or Voronoi tessellation are generated from a point distribution. Each point location of a dataset is enclosed by one discrete polygon. The same polygon also contains all the land that is closer to that point than any other. Distance can be calculated according to different metric spaces but usually in the Euclidean space. The boundary between two polygons falls at the midpoint of the distance between their defining points. In order to calculate the boundary arc of a certain polygon, straight lines are drawn between the defining point and its neighbouring ones. Then, by projecting perpendicular lines from the midpoints, the polygon is formed with peaks at the intersection of these lines (Pearce, 2000: 289; Wheatley & Gillings, 2002: 150; Conolly and Lake, 2006: 211; Halls et al 2001: 106).

Thiessen polygons have been used in a number of different applications in the social and environmental sciences, as they have in archaeology since the late 1960's. Applications were intended to investigate territoriality with selected archaeological entities acting as the centroids of polygons. In this way, all locations within each polygon belonged to the realm of each centroid, which was assumed to have exercised some kind of influence upon them. As a result, Thiessen polygons were primarily used to study the sociopolitical environment of competition rather than environmentally determined catchments and to visualize levels of hierarchy (Ruggles & Church, 1996: 164; Savage, 1990: 351; Peregrine, 1995: 255; Lock & Harris, 1996: 223; Renfrew & Level, 1979; Soetens et al 2003; Claßen & Zimmermann, 2004: 469).

The decreasing use of tesselation at this time is attributed to its serious methodological shortcomings (Ruggles and Church, 1996: 150-164; Renfrew & Level, 1979: 146-151; Milner, 1996: 993; Wheatley and Gillings, 2002: 151, 183; Conolly and Lake, 2006: 211-213). One way to deal with some of them is to weigh the polygons by attributing to the points some quantity that differentiates them according to a specific criterion. However, the acknowledged subjectivity in determining the values of the variable to be used accounts for its limited use. Then why do I proceed with this methodology? A list of its disadvantages and why they have little effect on my case study is provided in Table 4.2.

Kriging

There is a wide variety of methods of interpolation in the international bibliography for the management of quantitative variables and the construction of continuous surface maps. Nearly all of them have been used in archaeological research. Kriging has to date been used to a limited extent in archaeology (Lloyd & Atkinson, 2004: 152) due to its particularly demanding character, both in terms of understanding its functions and the capacity of computers (Robinson & Zubrow, 1999: 70,79).

Nevertheless, recognising its many advantages, I chose Kriging for the present study. It is local, in other words, it recognises and takes patterns of spatial autocorrelation between neighbouring points into consideration. It is exact, because it maintains the data of the samples. The surface which arises is continuous (without steep slopes) and is constrained, in other words, it receives values from within a restricted range (Wheatley & Gillings, 2002: 184; Syllaios et al 2007: 106 f.f.; Contreras, 2009: 1012). Unlike other methods it is not affected by 'edge effects' (Robinson & Zubrow, 1999: 79, 82). Furthermore, it is the only method of spatial interpolation that yields estimates of the errors associated with interpolation and reveals weaknesses in the sampling strategy (Ebert, 2002: 88-89). This happens because, apart from the prediction surface, it also provides a variogram and a directional variogram to model how well each interpolated value fits the model determined by the user, but also the direction of influence of the spatial dependence of the points of the sample (Syllaios et al, 2007: 106; Bevan & Conolly, 2009: 958).

As there are many types of interpolation available with the use of geostatistics, the application of a series of different types can lead to the adoption of the most suitable model. The steps which are followed in the application can be summarised as follows (Ebert, 2002: 83-84):

- Understanding the distribution of data. If distribution is not normal, data needs to be transformed.
- Identification of the presence/ absence of a trend and subsequent trend removal (the trend will be added back before the final surface is produced).
- Understanding spatial autocorrelation and incorporating anisotropy into the model.
- Defining neighborhood.
- Cross-validation: This is the most crucial step of the procedure because it demonstrates how well the choices in the previous steps work. Several methods for assessing a model's performance exist (Verhagen, 2009: 92-93) bearing in mind that there are no perfect models and the element of 'prediction error' is always present.

Table 4.2: Characteristics of Thiessen Polygons and their application in the present study.

GENERAL DISADVANTAGES	CURRENT APPLICATION
All the available space is allocated to unique polygons, as if territorial authority occurs everywhere and there are no boundaries beyond which it does not occur.	The study area is the official City Plan of Patras, in which the jurisdiction of the building and archaeological legislation is continuous without exception. The boundaries of the model are the true boundaries of the study case.
All centroids are regarded contemporaneous, and equal. Issues of hierarchical arrangement are ignored.	All excavations are contemporaneous (dating from the period 2004-08) and non-overlapping. Excavations are treated equally despite variation in the size and no hierarchy is assumed.
It does not provide a continuous result unlike other interpolation procedures.	No continuous result is expected because the data belongs to the nominal scale of measurement.
It treats space between the points as featureless, and culturally and physically isotropic.	Space between excavation sites is indeed featureless, in the sense that the presence or absence of archaeology is unknown, until other excavations are carried out, and tessellation changes. The study area is not addressed as a physical anisotropic landscape, but rather as an administrative unit in which cultural isotropia is expressed as everyone's free right to move about and invest in land according to specific legislation.

The Geostatistical Analyst Wizard includes both cross-validation and validation tests. In addition, it calculates statistics for the prediction errors which can be used as diagnostics to determine the predictive power of a model (Johnston et al 2001: 34). Cross-validation is a type of internal testing that uses all the data to estimate the trend and the autocorrelation model. Validation is an external test that uses all the data of one dataset (training) to predict values for an independent dataset (test), of which we know the observed values.

- Comparing Models: At this stage the results of two predictive models are compared and the best is identified.

4.3.4 Tools of Statistics

The parallel use of different types of statistical tests apart from Spatial Analysis constitutes a system of checks and balances to crosscheck and understand the statistical significance of spatial phenomena. For this reason, many researchers turn to a combination of tests of classical and spatial statistics, in order to achieve greater reliability in the validation of the statistical significance of their data and proceed to qualitative interpretation (Harris & Lock, 1990; Kvamme, 1995: 7; Higginbottom et al 2002: 54). The choice of statistical test depends on the scale on which each variable is measured, on the number of sample groups which participate in each test, the number of observations in each sample and whether they are normally distributed (Shennan, 1988· Drennan, 1996).

More specifically, the x^2, Mann Whitney and Kruskal Wallis tests were used. When they were being run, it was ascertained whether the difference between the data of the samples was random, in other words, whether there is no difference (Null Hypothesis is true) or is significant (disproving Null Hypothesis) on a specific level of significance, α, which in archaeological literature is usually defined as 0.05 (Drennan, 1996:160). This means that the Null Hypothesis is disproved if the data is so unusual that the probability p, the result that the statistical test yields randomly, is equal to or lower than 5% (Shennan, 1988: 49-53; Drennan, 1996: 160-162). In other words:

if p≤α, then the Null Hypothesis is true
if p>α, then the Null Hypothesis is disproved.

X² test

This test is used to correlate two or more nominal (categorical) variables. These variables include the age of antiquities, the type of archaeological finds, the preservation status of the finds, the existence of archaeological or non-archaeological surfaces in the City Plan, etc. The one-sample (one-way) test was selected, in which the real frequencies of a variable in every city planning zone are compared with the expected frequencies if the distribution of a variable in the study area was uniform (Shennan, 1988: 65). The one-sample test overcomes many of the difficulties related to the testing of two samples as it treats the population as stable. The samples compared with that

population show that they are unusual or deviant. In other words, the one-sample tests explore the local variance in a sample, while the population is regarded as given (Shennan, 1988: 65-70; Kvamme, 1990b: 369).

Occasionally, the x^2 test cannot yield reliable results, and this happens when: a) an expected value is less than 1, or b) 20% of all the expected values of a test are less than 5 (Drennan, 1996: 197). In these cases Fisher's exact probability test was applied as an alternative (Drennan, 1996: 197-8; Wansleeben & Verhart, 1995: 160) along with the Monte Carlo simulation (Aldenderfer, 1998: 110-111; Fisher et al 1997: 585; Conolly & Lake, 2006: 161-2).

In practice, x^2 assesses the deviation of the observed values from the expected ones (Drennan, 1996: 188-9). In order for this test to take place for categorical 'city planning' variables, the proportion of the whole study area which corresponds to each City Plan zone has been calculated.

In particular, for the calculation of the surface area of the City Plan in cells, GIS was used. The thematic database was georeferenced with the digital map of the City Plan. The existing vector structure of the map was transformed into raster. In this way, the study area was divided into a series of discrete spatial units of equal size, that is, the cells, which constitute the whole of the area, just as a mosaic consists of separate tiles. In each cell is stored data which represents the properties of the object which it describes as well as its geographical coordinates. It is, in other words, stored data which concerns the geographical space which it portrays (Pappas, 2011: 132-133; Kvamme, 1990b: 370-371). In order for the surface area of the buildable zone to be measured, the cells which are located in that zone were counted, as were those in the zone of public spaces. The total surface area constitutes the sum of the cells in the two zones.

Mann-Whitney and Kruskal-Wallis

These tests are used to correlate variables which are at least qualitative and can be classified, that is, they can be arranged in ascending order (Papadimas & Koilias, 1998: 47). In addition, they can be used to correlate quantitative continuous variables, when the necessary prerequisites are not met for using parametric statistical tests, e.g. the T-test and ANOVA. The necessary prerequisites are not met when the values of the variable do not follow the normal distribution, and also when the samples that are correlated do not have equal standard deviation (Blalock, 1979: 336). Tests of this type are called non-parametric, because they do not take into consideration the parameters of the values of the variable. These tests compare the median values of samples and not their arithmetic means, as happens with parametric tests.

The median value of a sample, that is, of a group of observations, is the middle observation. In relation to the median value, half of the observations are smaller or equal and the other half are bigger (Papadimas & Koilias,

1998:127). The median constitutes a representative measure of location of a sample, especially when the sample contains a very small number of outliers in one direction of the distribution (Blalock, 1979: 67; Shennan, 1988: 44).

With the Mann-Whitney test the medians of two samples of the same variable are compared. The Null Hypothesis states that median values do not differ from each other.

If the probability is greater than the level of statistical significance ($p>\alpha$), the Null Hypothesis is true and whatever differences exist between the samples are considered random in the context of sampling. If, however, the Null Hypothesis is disproved, then there is a statistically significant difference between the distributions of the samples.

The process which is followed is for the two groups to be combined into one big group, and all the observations to be entered into this unified group and to occupy a position in ascending order. Observations are then ranked from lowest to highest. These rankings are then resorted into the two separate samples. Then, the observed sum of ranks for each sample is calculated. If the two sums are almost equal, then they originate from the same population (Hasenstab, 1996: 232; Mink et al 2006: 228-229).

A very similar procedure is followed for the Kruskall Wallis test, with the difference that it is run when three or more samples of the same variable are examined. The Null Hypothesis states that the samples originate from the same population (Blalock, 1979: 368-369).

In the present application these tests will be used to correlate quantitative data which originates from excavations in Patras in various zones of the City Plan for which it was not possible to conduct parametric tests.

Chapter 5

Application and Results

In the following chapter a series of applications are implemented in the context of quantitative research, the results of which are then presented. First of all, the distribution of the sample was tested in order to determine whether the sample was representative of the construction activity of the area in general or whether it was biased geographically towards one area at the expense of another. Subsequently, a predictive model was created of potential archaeological sites throughout the City Plan area using Thiessen polygons. Next, with the method of Local Spatial Autocorrelation any clusters or outliers of the sample were detected, in order to see what they consisted of, in what way they influenced the model and for what reasons.

The reliability of the model, which was ensured by the Thiessen technique based on a sample of excavations from a five-year period, was evaluated by comparing that surface with the published archaeological map of the city. The two maps originated from two different sources. The Thiessen polygons were derived from data concerning 947 excavations in the period 2004-2008. The archaeological map was based on the findings of all the studies which were carried out by the Archaeological Service up to the beginning of the 21st century.

Since the conclusions were positive regarding the reliability of the model, other variables were examined so as to enhance it, such as the delay until the end of the rescue excavation, voluntary private funding and the maximum known depth without archaeological deposits. Then, the most suitable variable was selected. The Kriging method was used to create a continuous surface model, which depicted the predictive model of maximum depth without archaeological deposits. A combination of the two predictive models, (that is, the model of potential archaeological surface and the model of maximum depth without archaeological deposits) generated a unified model containing both sets of information, in other words, the areas of Patras where it is speculated that archaeological strata exist, as well as the estimated depth of the archaeological horizon, which coincides with the maximum known depth without archaeology in those areas.

This knowledge is useful because it can be utilised practically when incorporated into the city planning procedure, particularly when determining building regulations. For this reason, in the final phase of the application the specific characteristics of the excavations, e.g. archaeological or non-archaeological, date and type of archaeological finds, intended depth of excavation, potential archaeological surfaces, etc., were correlated with the existing building regulations and relationships were sought, which, though invisible, have an impact on the fate of unearthed antiquities, as well as the completion of construction works in the city.

5.1 Testing the distribution of the sample

The first step was to test the sample of excavations, so as to determine whether it is representative of the construction activity in the area in general or whether it is biased geographically towards one area at the expense of another.

To this end, the map of buildings produced by the Statistical Service for its 2001 survey was used as a reference backgound (Fig. 4.1). In that year 37,424 buildings were recorded within the boundaries of the approved City Plan. The distribution of the 947 excavations which were recorded in the same area during the period 2004-08 (Fig. 4.4) was compared with the distribution of those buildings.

In order to make this comparison, the area was divided into four zones: the northern, the southern, the central and the eastern, which correspond to the four municipal districts of the city.

For each zone the following was found:

- the mean centre of each distribution
- the standard distance of the data of each distribution from its mean centre (Augspurger & Franson, 1987; Thapar et al 1999; Nye et al 2009) (Fig. 5.1).

The data collected was tested statistically with the x^2 test. The Null Hypothesis stated that there is no difference between the distributions of the two samples, that is, of the total number of buildings of each zone in the city in 2001 and the excavations in the same zones in the period 2004-2008. Since the test did not yield statistically significant results ($p > \alpha$, $\alpha = 0.05$), the Null Hypothesis is true (Table 5.1).

Despite the large numerical difference which distinguishes the two populations, the centroids of their distributions are very close and their dispersal is similar, as is the size of their standard deviation. Consequently, the distribution of excavations can be considered to be representative of the general distribution of completed buildings in the city and does not appear to conceal some kind of dependence, which would be a hindrance to its further exploitation, such as in the applications that follow.

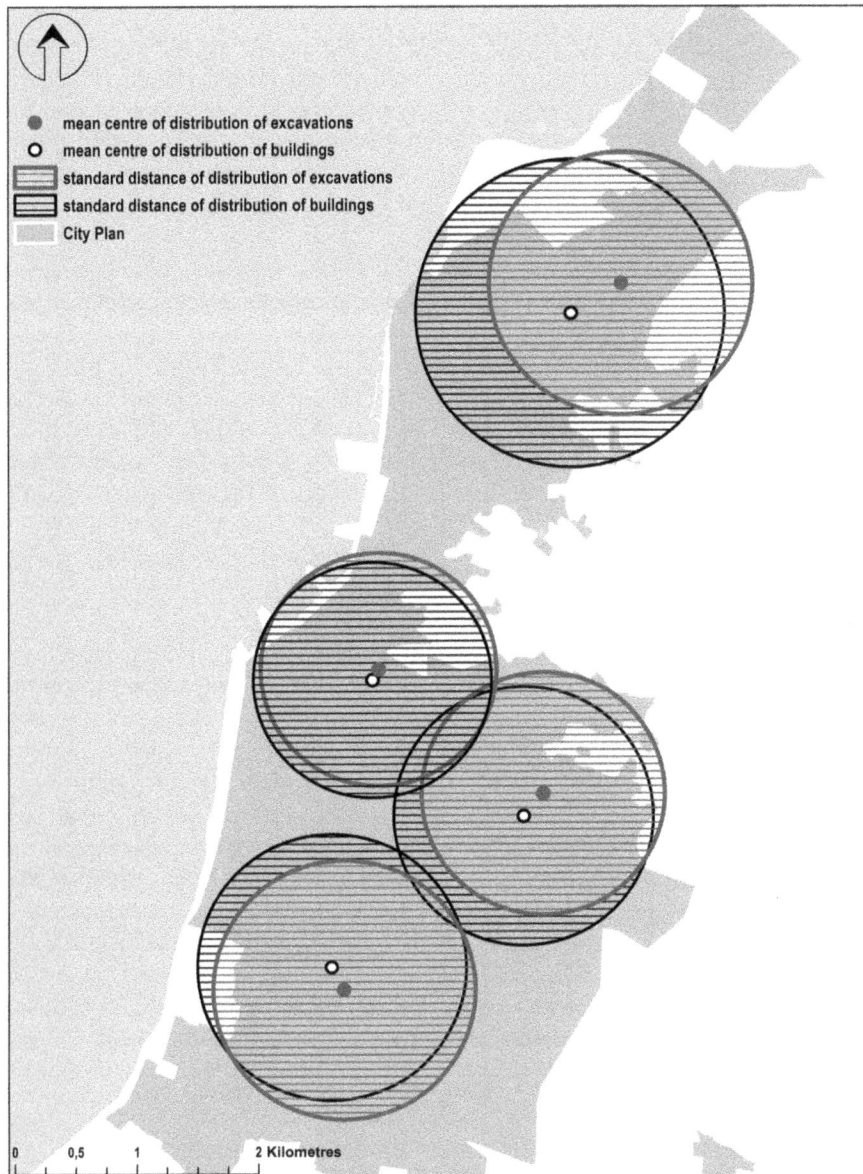

Fig. 5.1: Standard distances of excavations and buildings from their mean centres in the four zones of the city.

5.2 Predictive modelling of archaeological potential

This chapter puts forward a method for understanding and estimating the archaeological potential of every new excavation in a city based on the reports of past excavations and is followed by a discussion as to how the results correspond to the known archaeological pattern of the city. The rationale behind the application is that those entities nearer to an entity with a known characteristic (in

our case presence/absence of archaeology) are more likely to demonstrate a related characteristic than those further away, which is referred to as the 'First Law of Geography' (Tobler, 1970). To this end, Thiessen polygons are used.

5.2.1 Thiessen Polygons

The present application makes use only of the information regarding the absence/presence of archaeology, which is

Table 5.1: Numerical data associated with Fig. 5.1.

| | Coordinates of Mean centre | | | | Standard distance (m) | |
| | x | | y | | Radius = 1 st dev | |
	Buildings 2001	Excavations 2004-8	Buildings 2001	Excavations 2004-8	Buildings 2001	Excavations 2004-8
North	303547.7	303961.6	4237942.6	4238189	1271.7	1085.5
South	301589.7	301691	4234912.9	4232350.7	1098.2	1070.4
Central	301922.6	301973.5	4232538.6	4235000.6	971	961.4
Eastern	303159	303319.5	4233788.3	4233973.9	1068.3	1000.8
x^2 (α=0.05)	p=0.988		p=0.9997		p=0.0607	

Table 5.2: Frequency table of the excavations

	2004	2005	2006	2007	2008	Total
Archaeological Excavations	16	24	68	15	19	142
Non-Archaeological Excavations	144	165	302	101	87	799
Total	160	189	370	116	106	**941**

the commonest found in all excavation reports. A set of reports dating from between 2004 and 2008 were used. The database contained 941 records, each corresponding to a single excavation, either on a plot of land or within the road network. The database was connected to a map of the City Plan of Patras and 941 points representing the excavation sites were digitised (Table 5.2).

By creating Thiessen polygons for each year's excavations, it was possible to compare the space allocated to the archaeological or non-archaeological points of one year with the excavated sites of the following year and examine to what extent the latter are found within this space. Thiessen polygons were generated from points representing the excavations of the case study. The point pattern for every year was used and points were converted into Thiessen polygons. The output coverage inherited that part of the point attribute table which contained the information on the absence or presence of archaeological finds at each of the excavation sites. The point distribution for each year's excavations was overlaid on the cumulative tessellation of the previous year's excavations (Table 5.3).

Their predictive strength was tested over a period of five years, by calculating the percentage of 'correct predictions'

that occurred every year, namely, archaeological excavations in cumulative archaeological tessellation and non-archaeological excavations in cumulative non-archaeological tessellation. In this way it was possible to test how indicative the tesselation map is of the probability of archaeological discovery or not during any ground disturbance activity in the city.

The 2005 point distribution was then superimposed on the polygons generated for the 2004 excavation pattern (Figure 5.2, top left)

The 2006 point distribution was laid over the polygons of both the 2004 and 2005 patterns (Figure 5.2, top right) and so on (Figure 5.2, bottom). Thus, for each year the tessellation of the pattern of the soil removal areas was adjusted and updated according to new evidence. The space allocated to archaeology nearly always ranged from 5 to 6% (Table 5.4).

If the excavations of both types were uniformly distributed in the space, then the polygons would present a uniformity in size and shape. This is not the case and many polygons seem to form clusters with neighbouring ones. Furthermore, if the two types of excavations for each year were not connected with the archaeological and non-archaeological polygons of the previous years, their distribution would be uniform in the whole area. In other words, the same density of excavations would be expected. For example, if this were the case, then the points of 5.47% of the excavations of 2005 would be contained in the archaeological polygons of 2004, because the latter constituted 5.47% of the total area. Instead, 12.17% of all the excavations are found there. Moreover, 29.17% of the archaeological excavations

Table 5.3: Excavations in cumulative Thiessen polygons of the previous years' excavations*

	2005 excavations in 2004 polygons	2006 excavations in 2004-2005 polygons	2007 excavations in 2004-2006 polygons	2008 excavations in 2004-2007 polygons	Total
Archaeological excavations in archaeological polygons	7/24 (29.17%)	15/68 (22.06%)	9/15 (60%)	13/19 (68.42%)	44/126 (34.92%)
Archaeological excavations in non-archaeological polygons	17/24 (70.83%)	53/68 (77.94%)	6/15 (40%)	6/19 (31.58%)	82/126 (65.08%)
Non-archaeological excavations in non-archaeological polygons	149/165 (90.30%)	289/302 (95.70%)	88/101 (87.13%)	81/87 (93.10%)	607/655 (92.67%)
Non-archaeological excavations in archaeological polygons	16/165 (9.70%)	13/302 (4.3%)	13/101 (12.87%)	6/87 (6.89%)	48/655 (7.33%)
Correct predictions	156/189 (82.54%)	304/370 (82.16%)	97/116 (83.62%)	94/106 (88.68%)	651/781 (83.35%)

Year 2004 is omitted in the table since it was the first year of the project.

Table 5.4: Proportion of the study area allocated to polygons

	2004	2004-5	2004-6	2004-7	2004-8
Archaeological polygons	5.47%	4.21%	5.73%	5.30%	5.48%
Non-archaeological polygons	94.53%	95.79%	94.27%	94.70%	94.52%

Table 5.5: Fisher's Exact Probability test values obtained from data in Table 5.3.

	2005	2006	2007	2008
criteria	2005 excavations and 2004 polygons	2006 excavations and 2004-05 polygons	2007 excavations and 2004-06 polygons	2008 excavations and 2004-07 polygons
p	0.014	<0.0005	<0.0005	<0.0005
α	0.05	0.05	0.05	0.05

and only 9.70% of the non-archaeological excavations are contained in the archaeological polygons of the previous years (Table 5.3).

2005 was just the second year of the project and therefore the 189 excavations of the database could only be compared with the 160 of the previous year, of which only 16 were archaeological sites. As a result, there is a poor coverage of the archaeological digs of 2005 by the archaeological tessellation of 2004. Only one third of the archaeological sites lie in the archaeological polygons of 2004. Yet the distribution of excavations in 2005 is not totally random with regard to what we know from 2004. Indeed, only 9.70% of the non-archaeological excavations lie in the archaeological polygons of 2004. In addition, the overall percentage of 'correct predictions' is as high as 82.54%. The area covered by archaeological polygons in 2004 represents 5.78% of the total area.

Apparently, the archaeological tessellation of one year is by no means sufficient. As soon as more data was introduced into the database, the picture became clearer. In the following year the building activity increased and 370 recorded sites in Patras underwent soil removal, 21 more than those of 2004 and 2005 combined. Despite the high number, the location of the sites tends to comply with the pattern formed by the 2004-2005 Thiessen polygons. Out of 68 archaeological excavations 77.94% lie outside archaeological polygons and 4.3% of the non-archaeological excavations are to be found inside archaeological polygons. 22.06% of the archaeological excavations lie in archaeological polygons and 95.70% of the non-archaeological digs lie in non-archaeological polygons, making 82.16% of the total predictions correct. In 2007, the third year of the application, correct predictions for archaeological excavations jump to 60%, and the next year they reach 68%. Year by year the predictive strength of cumulative tessellation is dynamically improving.

5.2.2 Further statistical and spatial analysis

Visual inspection was complemented with the employment of statistical tests, x^2 and Fisher's Exact Probability, to further test the hypothesis that every year's new rescue excavations and already established archaeological tessellation are not independently located. Then, Kvamme's Gain Statistic was calculated. The few exceptions of false predictions, though they decrease gradually, needed identification and review. For this reason, Local Moran's I, was run to identify statistically significant clusters and outliers. The outliers are particularly interesting, because they concern the existence of archaeological excavations surrounded by non-archaeological ones and vice versa.

For the statistical analysis the data was classified according to two criteria (presence/ absence of archaeological deposits in the excavation sites and the type of polygon, archaeological or non-archaeological, in which they lie) and four tests were run on how independent the classes are (Shennan, 1988: 70). Independence of the classes represents the Null Hypothesis. The x^2 test was employed first. The results were not always statistically valid, because expected frequencies were below the threshold of 5, a strict limit for one degree of freedom. In that case, Fisher's exact probability test was performed, which constitutes a direct calculation of the significance probability with no requirements on the expected values, usually performed when x^2 is not valid (Drennan, 1996:197-8; Wansleeben & Verhart, 1995: 160).

The Null Hypothesis was disproved, and there is an extremely low probability that differences between the two criteria have been caused by chance (Table 5.5).

Kvamme's Gain Statistic determines the predictive capability of a model, by comparing the proportion of the surface which is occupied by the potential archaeological

Table 5.6: Kvamme's Gain Statistic values obtained from data in Tables 5.3 and 5.4.

	2005	2006	2007	2008
criterion 1	% surface of 2004 archaeological polygons	% surface of 2004-05 archaeological polygons	% surface of 2004-06 archaeological polygons	% surface of 2004-07 archaeological polygons
criterion 2	% 2005 archaeol. excavations in 2004 archaeol. polygons	% 2006 archaeol. excavations in 2004-05 archaeol. polygons	% 2007 archaeol. excavations in 2004-06 archaeol. polygons	% 2008 archaeol. excavations in 2004-07 archaeol. polygons
Formula	G= 1-(%surface/%points)			
G	0.81	0.8	0.9	0.92

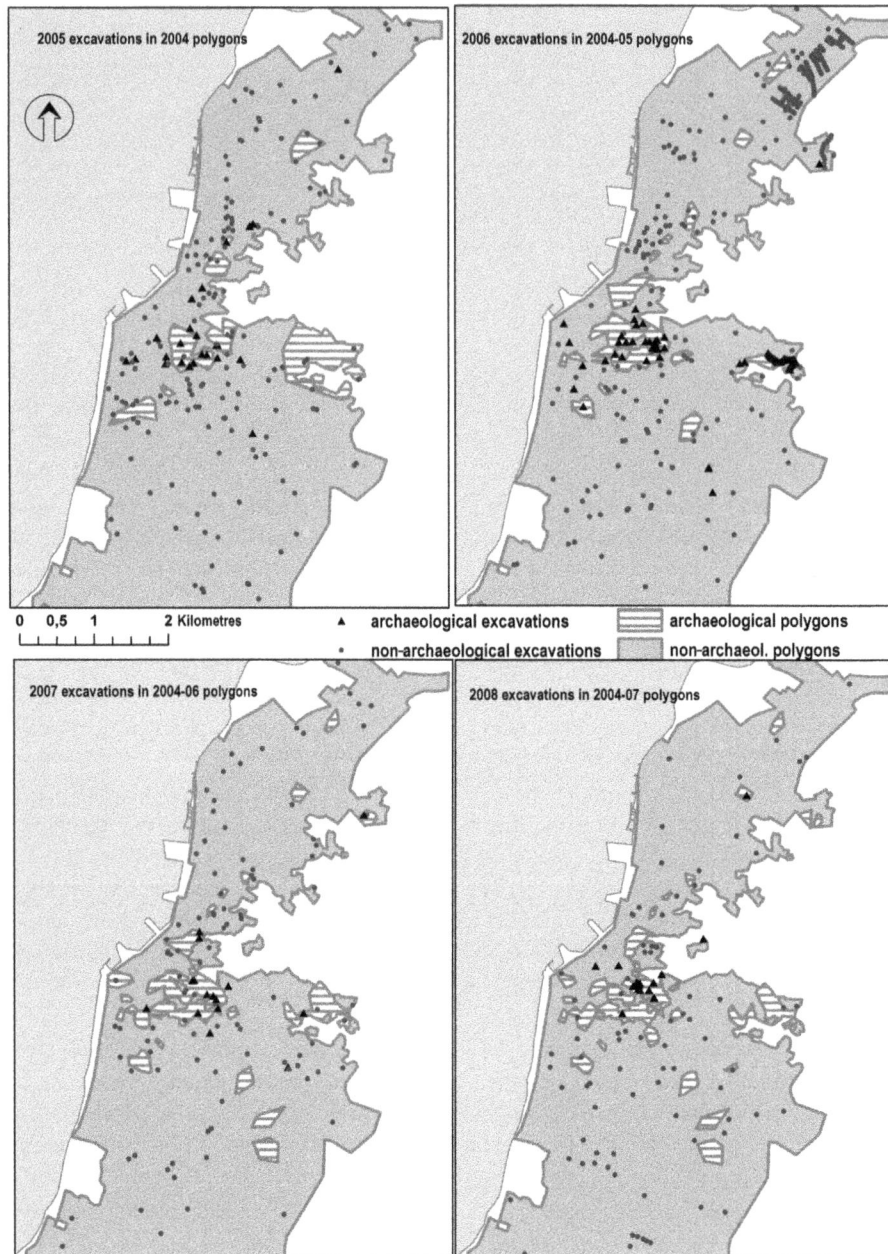

Fig. 5.2: The Thiessen polygons and the distribution of the excavations.

polygons with the proportion of correct predictions from an independent sample of points. Values close to 1 show that the model can be used for predictions of potential archaeological polygons. This happens when one (as large as possible) proportion of the independent sample falls within a (as small as possible) proportion of the total surface of the model (Kvamme, 1988; Mink et al 2006: 233-236; Westcott & Kuiper, 2000: 69; Verhagen, 2009: 76). Indeed, the Kvamme's Gain Statistic for potential archaeological surface for 2004-2007 compared with the archaeological excavations of 2008 yielded a value of G= 0.92 (Table 5.6).

An additional spatial statistical test was performed to facilitate data analysis and interpretation at a localized level (Kvamme, 1993: 91). Local Moran's I test (Invert Distance/Euclidean Distance) was selected due to the need to detect clusters of excavation sites with similar values

(archaeological or non-archaeological) and sites with values different from their neighbours, that is, archaeological sites in close proximity to non-archaeological ones and vice versa. This type of analysis would not have been possible with the application of global spatial autocorrelation tests (Premo, 2004: 856-857; Chiang & Liu, 2012: 299-300).

The resulting index shows that whilst non-archaeological sites form no clusters, the archaeological ones are clustered (Figure 5.3).

The clusters correspond to the archaeological pattern configured by tessellation (Figure 5.4).

However, 10 archaeological sites were surrounded by non-archaeological ones and 42 non-archaeological sites were inside or very close to archaeological clusters. The

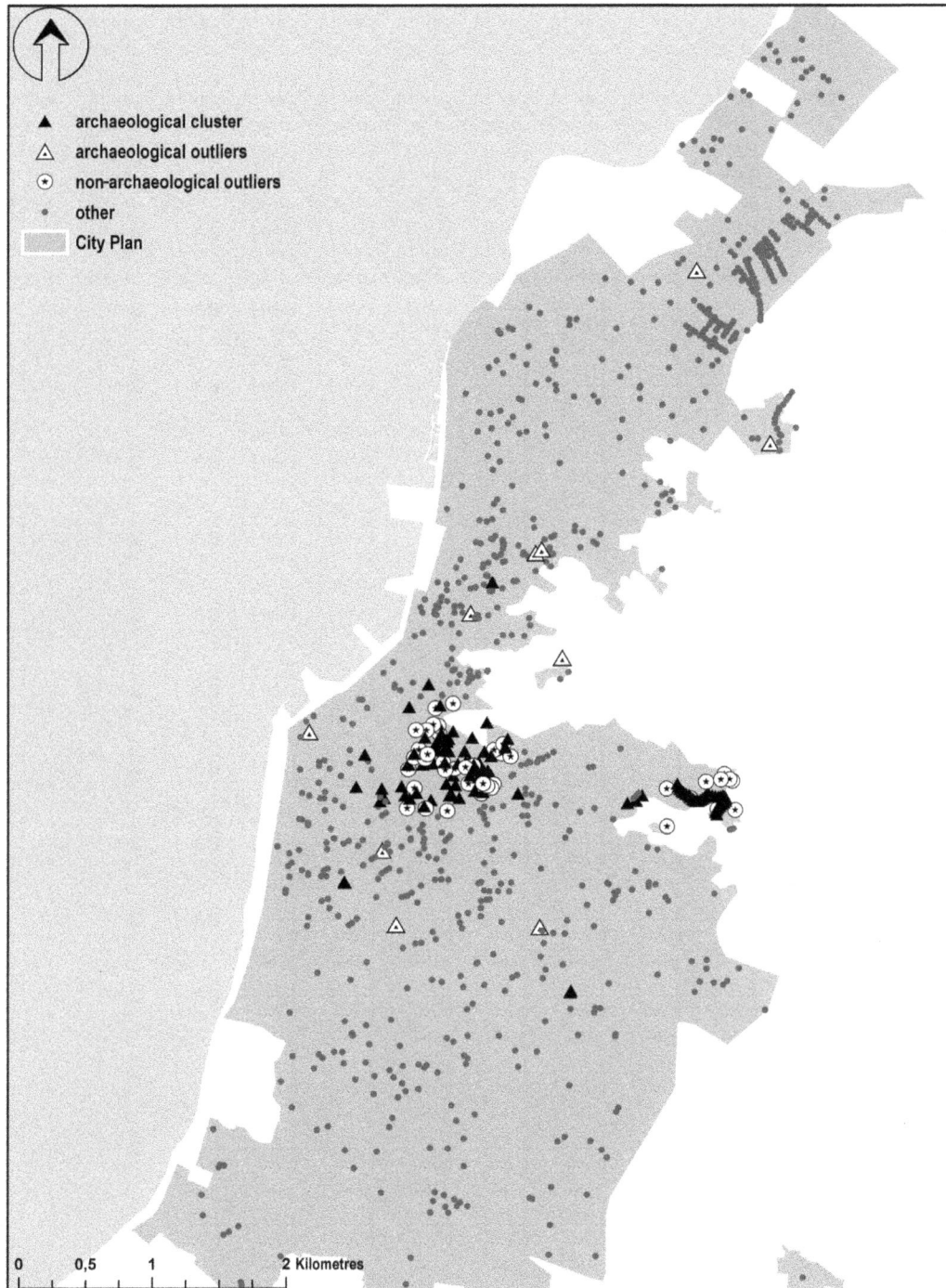

Fig. 5.3: Clusters and outliers according to the Local Moran's I test.

existence of statistically significant (0.05 level) outliers, both archaeological and non-archaeological, merits further study and interpretation in conjunction with background contextual information.

5.2.3 Results and Discussion

It is possible, therefore, to compare the results of the application with prior knowledge and see to what extent they match. The tessellation of 2004 already gives insights into the archaeological profile. The configuration of the archaeological polygons changes as more excavations are included. It is worth noting that even though the tessellation of

2004-8 was made up of 941 excavations, the archaeological space they occupy still accounts for 5.48% of the total area, a proportion equal to that of the archaeological space in 2004 which contained 160 excavation sites (Table 5.4). Every time the dataset increases, less space is allocated to each site. The archaeological space becomes more compact and the boundaries of the pattern are revealed in greater detail. Special function areas and outliers begin to show up like islands.

The completion of the current application is depicted on the map in Figure 5.4. The residential and artisanal areas of the Classical, Hellenistic, Roman and Byzantine periods

35

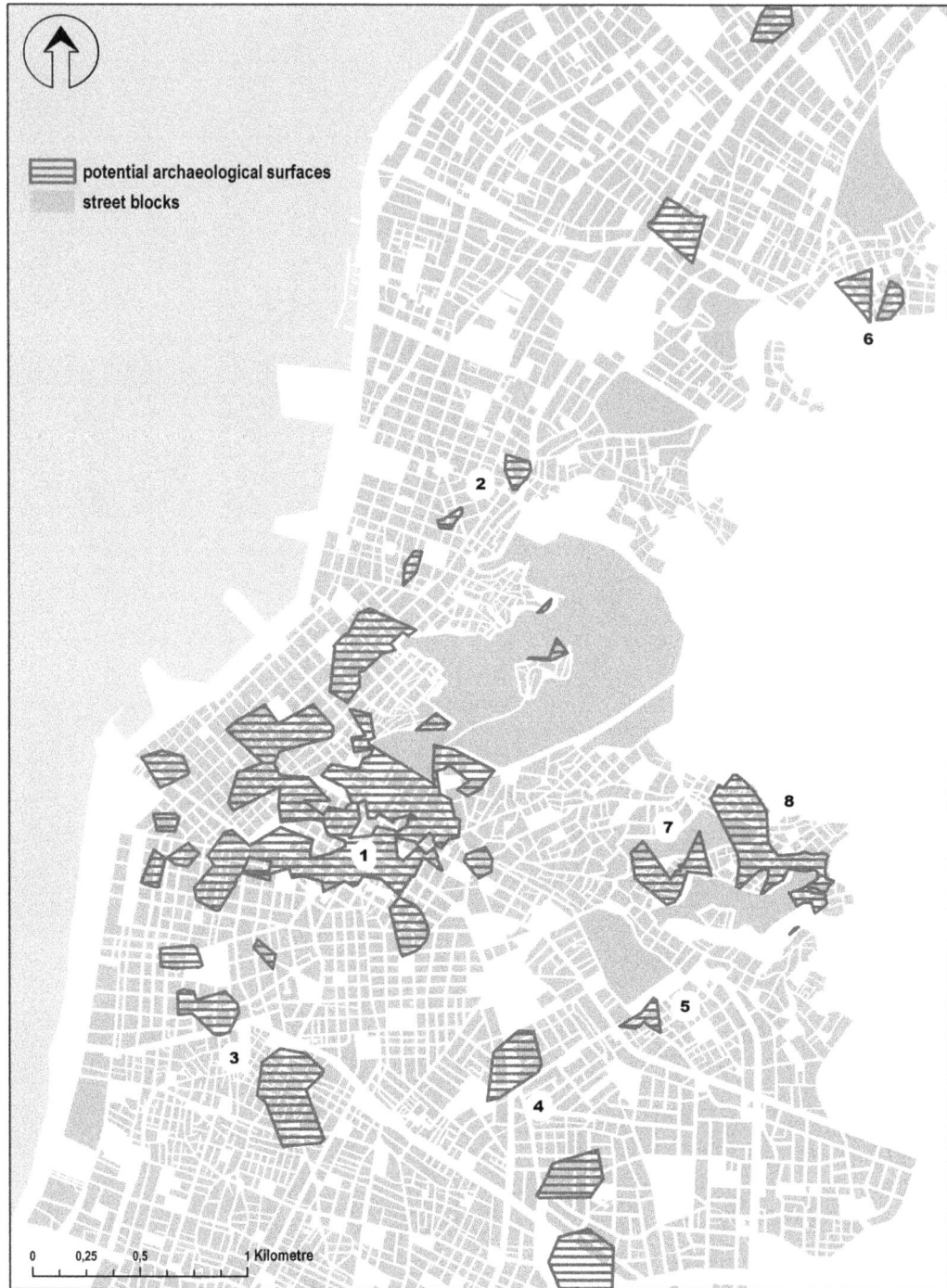

Fig. 5.4: Potential archaeological surfaces in the City Plan based on the excavations during the period 2004-08.

are all located in the biggest archaeological polygon of the application (Fig. 5.4: no. 1). Public buildings and private houses, workshops and infrastructure were discovered during excavations. A few burial sites were also discovered bearing witness to small cemeteries that had existed there (Lambropoulou & Moutzali, 2005: 63). The western parts of the polygon are occupied by the industrial zone (Rizakis & Petropoulos, 2005: 33).

From there the 'line' to the northeast, which is formed by 6 polygons, 4 closer to the city and 2 further away (Fig. 5.4: no. 2), is evidence of one of the three major ancient cemeteries, the northern one lying along the ancient road to

Corinth. Not all excavations here have led to the discovery of burial sites. However, it is known that outside the city there were several villae rusticae of both Roman and later periods, the owners of which preferred locations near roads, for easy transportation and communication (Stavropoulou Gatsi et al 2006: 95-99; Lambropoulou & Moutzali, 2005: 60).

The same picture appears where the other two major road axes and cemeteries lie, i.e. in the southwest and the southeast. The tessellation of 2004 generates polygons related to the southwestern cemetery. But by 2008 more excavations had produced archaeological finds, such as graves, vestiges of buildings, etc., and more archaeological polygons emerge (Fig. 5.4: no. 3). That makes sense because this is the area closest to the harbour and a lot of activity and commercial transactions took place there (Stavropoulou Gatsi et al 2006: 95; Lambropoulou & Moutzali, 2005: 70-71).

The line of the southeastern road that led to the hinterland of the Peloponnese and the southeastern cemetery is clearly shown crossing four polygons (Fig. 5.4: no. 4). A fifth polygon (Fig. 5.4: no. 5) going off at an angle from the line to the east might well be another villa rustica or a workshop outside the city (Stavropoulou Gatsi et al 2006: 95; Lambropoulou & Moutzali, 2005: 71). Two polygons to the northeastern edge of the map (Fig. 5.4: no. 6) and one polygon to the east (Fig. 5.4: no. 7) are located in two different zones of prehistoric habitation of the Bronze Age (Rizakis & Petropoulos, 2005: 6-7; Stavropoulou Gatsi et al 2006: 83-84). The latter is near a larger polygon at the edge of the City Plan where a Roman road was discovered (Fig. 5.4: no. 8).

Further consideration should be given to the 42 non-archaeological outliers inside or adjacent to archaeological clusters (Figure 5.3). In order to justify their existence it is necessary to refer to the history and documentation of each corresponding site. Four possible explanations are provided.

- *Difference in intended excavation depth:* e.g. one non-archaeological excavation site lies close to an archaeological one. The former had an excavation depth of 1 metre, whereas at the latter, which had a greater excavation depth, antiquities were found 1.40m below the road surface. Ten other similar cases were detected.
- *Proximity to an ancient road:* To this category belong 10 non-archaeological excavations which are adjacent to an archaeological cluster, which consists of excavations along a modern road located on top of an ancient one (Fig. 5.4: no. 8). In this area there will need to be more excavations nearer the ancient road in the future, in order to determine the use of the road during ancient times and the potential archaeological character of the neighbourhood.
- *Destruction of archaeological record at an earlier time:* Needless to say, the majority of the non-archaeological outliers belong to this group. Continuous habitation of the old city of Patras, along with natural and anthropogenic destruction throughout the centuries, has resulted in the disappearance of archaeological deposits.
- *Insufficient documentation and lack of publications:* The fact that documentation of excavations for other than research purposes started only recently is also to blame, as well as the fact that publication of rescue excavations for an unknown number of outliers is sparse and lacking in detail.

In addition, the coincidental absence of other archaeological excavations in the proximity of the sample plays a role. In two cases it can be said that it is a question of isolated finds in the sense that they concern a farmhouse and a part of an ancient road, without other information being known.

5.2.4 Conclusion

Excavations constitute a fast and functional way to record the archaeological palimpsest buried underneath modern cities. Recording and statistically processing information generated by the excavations of five consecutive years can significantly contribute to the configuration of a predictive archaeological model of a city, even if no prior knowledge is taken into account. Thiessen tessellation, classical statistics and spatial autocorrelation tests may complement each other and enhance each other's predictive potential. Complementary use of background information and the continuous updating of the dataset with more sites can minimise the frustration that unexpected outliers cause.

Lastly, it is worth emphasising that the only feature that was used in this application was the presence/absence of antiquities at each excavation. However, the reports also include other information (e.g. intended excavation depth, depth without archaeological deposits) which, combined with other data from rescue excavations (e.g. chronology, typology, etc.), is more suitable for more advanced applications in the field of Spatial Technology.

5.3 Interpolation

In this section the construction of more advanced models is presented with the inclusion of more variables which characterise the study area during the period 2004-2008.

Despite the fact that planning permission is issued on numerous occasions every year and the earth-moving works they involve are inspected by wardens of the Archaeological Service, limited documentation exists on the likelihood of not finding archaeological features on a site at a certain depth. There is no evidence that stakeholders are actually informed or warned about the possibility of discovering archaeological resources on the site prior to investment. They also lack an estimate of the duration of archaeological interventions, the consequent delay and the likely cost.

Initially, the Kriging method and the test of spatial autocorrelation were run. At an earlier stage of this study, logistic regression had also been employed (Simoni, 2013), but it is no longer considered necessary. Using the Kriging method, an interpolated model was created, selecting the most suitable variable and rejecting the rest. Finally, this model was combined with the model of potential archaeological surfaces to generate a unified predictive model.

5.3.1 Spatial and geostatistical analysis

The three variables which were used were: 'delay until the end of the rescue excavation', 'voluntary private funding' and 'maximum known depth without archaeological

Table 5.7: Results of prediction error statistics for delay until the end of rescue excavation and number of excavations sites that form the samples.

PREDICTION ERROR	Cross Validation 2004-07	Cross Validation 2004-08
mean	-6,41	0,126
RMSE	44,25	40,59
SE	8,994	38,71
Mean st.	-0,6836	0,002295
RMSE st.	5,728	1,08
2004-07 excavations:	**training sample: 768**	
2004-08 excavations:	**training sample: 855**	
2008 excavations:	**test sample: 87**	

deposits'. The predictive strength of these variables was tested. The three variables constituted three representative examples of the decisive procedure of choosing potential predictors. In this particular case, the selection was challenging, because it was not based on environmental factors, but on anthropogenic factors closely related to individual attitudes and social and legislative constraints.

Delay until the end of the rescue excavation

The first variable to be interpolated was the delay in working days due to the involvement of the Archaeological Service in the soil removal process of both archaeological and non-archaeological excavations.

Firstly, the delay was calculated for both types of excavation. As was obvious in the case of the former, the delay lasted for more than one day, due to the start of the rescue excavation. On the other hand, in the case of non-archaeological excavations the delay was limited to one day, usually the first, on which the site was disturbed by earth moving machinery and the archaeological warden supervised the work.

The Kriging method was applied. The data from excavations of the period 2004-2007 formed the training sample. The 2008 dataset constituted the test sample. The results of the validation are given in Table 5.7.

The extent to which a model provides accurate predictions is examined according to the following criteria:

- The mean prediction error (mean) should be near 0.
- The mean standardised prediction error (mean st.) should be near 0 and near the mean prediction error.
- The average standard error (S.E.) should be close to the root-mean-square prediction error (RMSE).
- The root-mean-square standardised prediction error (RMSE st.) should be close to 1. (Johnston et al 2001: 35).

As is obvious, the criteria were not met. The model was not successful and the variable was not used as a predictor.

Voluntary private funding of archaeological research

The second variable was the voluntary private funding of archaeological research in low budget projects. Its spatial distribution was examined in case some meaningful pattern could be discerned. It should be borne in mind that archaeological work on public land is by law funded by the investor and certainly no prediction is required. Based on the results of Moran's I and Getis-Ord G (p>0.05) (Table 5.8), the variable did not qualify as a potential predictor.

Table 5.8: Results of Global Moran's I and Getis Ord General tests.

	Index	z	p	α=0.05
Global Moran's I	-0.03	-0.47	0.636	Random
Getis Ord. Gen. G	0.002	-1.21	0.225	Random

Table 5.9: Results of prediction error statistics for maximum known depth of non-archaeological deposits in all excavations and number of excavations that form the samples.

PREDICTION ERROR	Cross Validation 2004-07	Cross Validation 2004-08	Validation training sample 2004-07 test sample 2008
mean	0.04754	0.05376	-0.000878
RMSE	0.8811	0.8961	1.065
SE	1.258	1.273	1.231
Mean st.	0.01742	0.02358	-0.02524
RMSE st.	0.7769	0.7803	0.9256
2004-07 excavations:	**training sample: 827**		
2004-08 excavations:	**training sample: 923**		
2008 excavations:	**test sample: 92**		

Fig. 5.5: Predictive Model of maximum known depth of non-archaeological deposits in the City Plan of Patras, using the Kriging method, based on the excavations in the period 2004-2008.

Maximum known depth of non-archaeological deposits

The third variable employed was the maximum known depth of non-archaeological deposits in both archaeological and non-archaeological excavations.

Again, the Kriging method was applied. First, the intepolation used data from excavation sites (training sample) of the period 2004-2007 to estimate values at sites (test sample) unearthed in the following year. Next, data from the whole record of 2004-2008 was input for interpolation. The results of the validation are presented in Table 5.9.

Examining the first and final columns of Table 5.9, it is obvious that the validation and cross-validation of the sample yield satisfactory values that fit the criteria. The procedure was repeated using all the data from 2004 to 2008 as a training sample, which also met the criteria (Table 5.9, middle column). For the above-mentioned reasons the model can be used as a predictor.

Using the procedure which has just been described, two of the three variables did not qualify as potential predictors. On the other hand, 'maximum known depth of non-archaeological deposits' did qualify, which may prove to

excavations

archaeological excavations

non-archaeological excavations

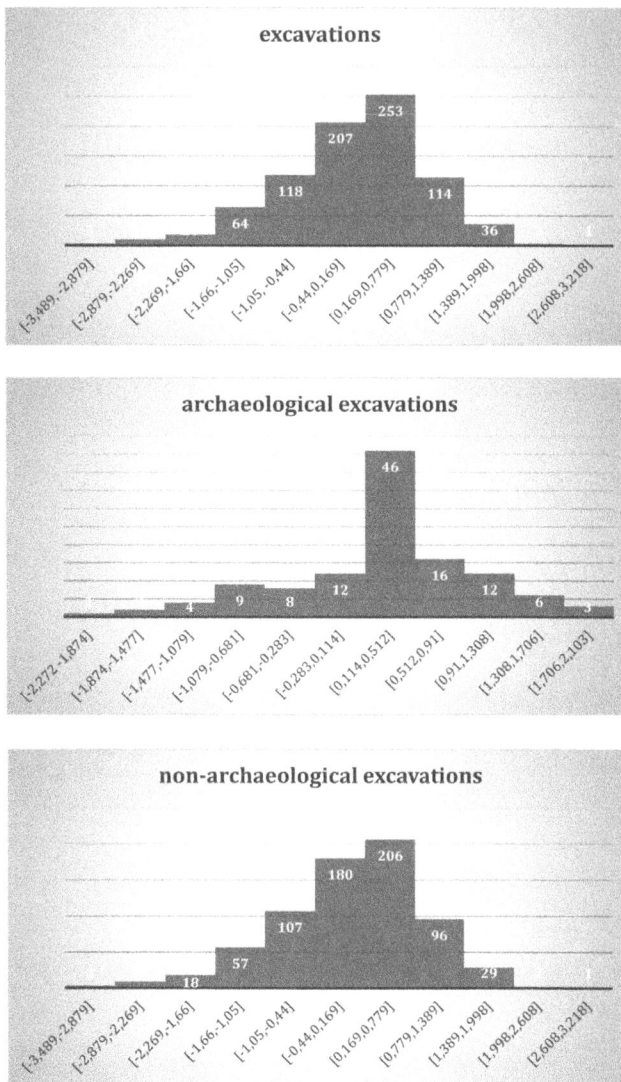

Fig. 5.6: Frequency distribution of prediction error for the predictive model 'maximum known depth without archaeological deposits' for 2004-07 from: a) all the excavations, b) the archaeological excavations and c) the non-archaeological excavations.

be a useful tool for those who wish to know how deep an excavation may go without putting buried antiquities at risk in any part of the city (Fig. 5.5).

5.3.2 Results

Before drawing any conclusions, it was necessary to analyse and understand the prediction error for maximum known depth without archaeological deposits. This was carried out in two steps: firstly using data from the excavations of 2004-

2007 and secondly using data from all the excavations, i.e. 2004-2008. Afterwards, the two models of the potential existence of antiquities (Fig.5.4) and maximum known depth without archaeological deposits (Fig. 5.5) were combined. The results are discussed below in the light of the known archaeological background of the city.

First, the data concerning the prediction error for the predictive model of maximum known depth without archaeological deposits for the excavations of 2004-2007 was explored. It was ascertained that the distribution of error is close to normal (Fig. 5.6).

Values greater than zero, which are in the majority (58%), represent the cases where the predicted depth was deeper than the observed one, whereas the values below zero represent the opposite cases. If only the data regarding the 119 archaeological excavations of the same period is examined, 75% of the sites show error with a positive sign, in other words, the archaeological horizon is found higher than was predicted, whereas with non-archaeological excavations the corresponding proportion is 56%.

The statistical properties of the distribution are summarised in Table 5.10. The mean error for archaeological excavations is far greater than the equivalent in all excavations and for the non-archaeological ones.

Although error is found in various locations in Patras, it mostly concerns isolated sites in the upper city. Why is this the case? It is known that this area has been continuously inhabited for thousands of years. This makes it difficult to make predictions for isolated sites, because the initial archaeological horizon of these sites may have been destroyed due to continuous construction activity or the archaeological horizon of neighbouring plots may have been destroyed. In addition, since the sample is based exclusively on the four-year period 2004-07, it can be improved by incorporating the data for the following year, as will be shown below. It is worth noting that the number of archaeological excavations that present error deviation of less than half a metre higher or lower was 63 (53%), whereas the corresponding figure for the non-archaeological excavations is 341 (48%). This means that for more than half of the archaeological sites a prediction with a difference of up to half a metre is possible.

Comparing the finds of 2008 with this model, it can be seen that of the 19 archaeological excavations of that year, only for six cases (located both in the upper and lower city)

Table 5.10: Summary statistics for the graph in Fig 5.6.

PREDICTION ERROR Dataset 2004-07 (maximum known depth without archaeological deposits)	All Excavations Count=827	Archaeolog. Excavations Count=119	Non- Archaeolog. Excavations Count=708
mean	0.05	0.2	0.01
Standard deviation	0.9	0.8	0.9
maximum	3.2	2.1	3.2
minimum	-3.5	-2.3	-3.5

excavations

archaeological excavations

non-archaeological excavations

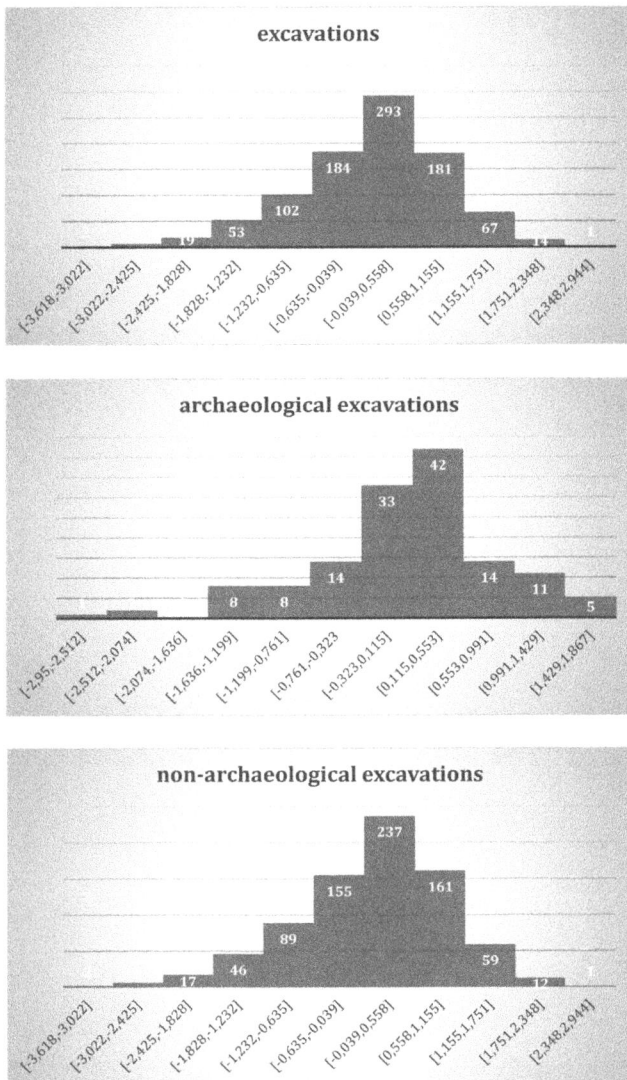

Fig. 5.7: Frequency distribution of prediction error for the predictive model 'maximum known depth without archaeological deposits' for the period 2004-08 from: a) all the excavations, b) the archaeological excavations and c) the non-archaeological excavations.

was there comparable data regarding depth, because the information concerning the others was missing. Conversely, of the 87 non-archaeological excavations only one lacked this piece of information. In terms of the archaeological sites, in three cases the difference between the maximum depth of non-archaeological deposits and the predicted depth was less than half a metre. In two other cases it was less than 1.5 metres and in one case it was 1.8 metres.

On the other hand, the data from the non-archaeological sites yielded no final maximum depth of non-archaeological deposits. In effect, the difference of the prediction from the real observations is not connected with the existence of antiquities (as they do not exist) and, theoretically, it would be possible to dig anywhere to any depth and not find antiquities if this particular area had not been in use in ancient times. As a consequence, these predictions are only useful for understanding the history of earth-moving works in the wider area of each site.

More specifically, differences greater than -2m are found at three separate sites where the depth was predicted to be less than the observed value, due to proximity to either archaeological excavations or non-archaeological excavations with a shallow intended excavation depth. A difference of 2m is found in only one case. Smaller differences with a positive or negative sign are few and far between and are also influenced by proximity to non-archaeological excavations with a shallow intended excavation depth.

Next, the data concerning the prediction error for the predictive model of maximum known depth without archaeological deposits for the excavations of 2004-08 was explored. It was not possible to validate this particular dataset, as no other data was available. Validation will be possible in the future, when the database has been enriched with more recent data.

The distribution of the prediction error for this model was also tested (Fig. 5.7) and is close to normal, the mean and median being 0.05m and 0.1m respectively. Of the 138 archaeological excavations, 90 sites (65%) show a difference of half a metre from the expected depth. The greatest difference is close to 3m and is found at sites in the heart of the upper city, where antiquities were detected at depths much greater than expected.

The prediction demonstrated that in 58% of the cases the predicted layer was much lower than what excavations revealed. An examination of only the data from the 138 archaeological excavations included in the sample reveals that at 60% of the sites, the archaeological horizon lies higher than predicted, whereas the corresponding proportion for non-archaeological excavations is 58%.

The mean prediction error for archaeological excavations is nearly the same as the corresponding figure for the total number of excavations and for non-archaeological

Table 5.11: Summary statistics for the graph in Figure 5.7.

PREDICTION ERROR Dataset 2004-08 (maximum known depth without archaeological deposits)	All Excavations Count=923	Archaeolog. Excavations Count=138	Non- Archaeolog. Excavations Count=785
mean	0.05	0.06	0.05
Standard deviation	0.9	0.8	0.9
maximum	2.9	1.9	2.9
minimum	-3.6	-2.9	-3.6

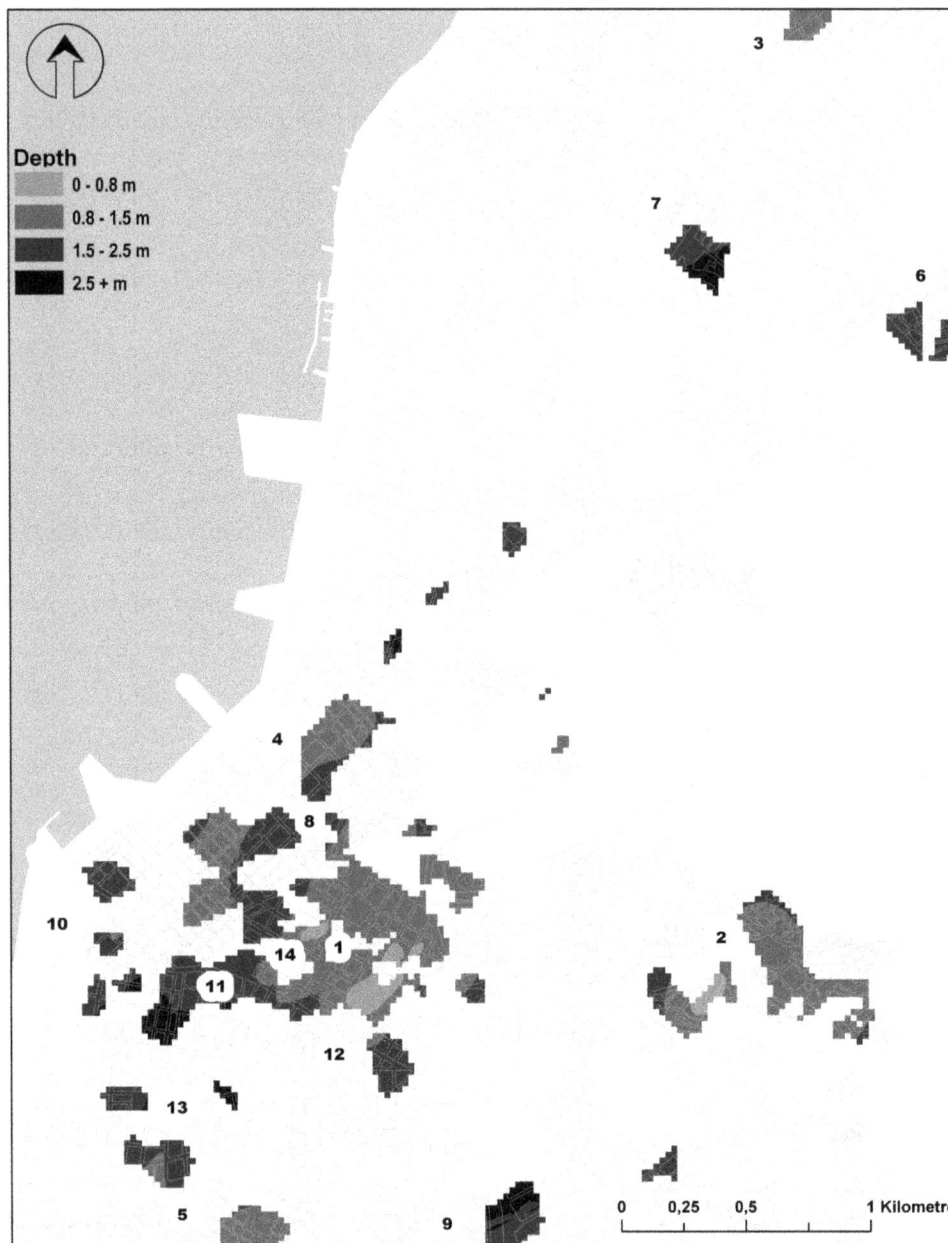

Fig. 5.8: Predictive Model of potential archaeological sites and potential minimum depth of discovery of an archaeological layer within the City Plan of Patras, using Thiessen Polygons and the Kriging method, based on the excavations of 2004-2008.

excavations, but with a slightly greater concentration around the mean (Table 5.11). With the addition of the data for 2008 the mean prediction error decreases compared to the corresponding figure for the years 2004-07.

Quantitatively, the values of prediction error that represent the ranges [minimum – standard deviation] and [standard deviation – maximum] are to be found at a small number of excavations, which for the archaeological sites is 42 (30%) and for non-archaeological sites is 158 (20%). In comparison to the corresponding figures for the period 2004-07 (33% and 31% respectively) these proportions show an improvement. In general, with this model the same restrictions apply as were referred to for the model of 2004-07, as well as for the Thiessen polygons model. This reminds us how complex and endless a procedure the

generation of a predictive model is, and that the production of every new predictive surface constitutes not the end of the work but the starting point for the enrichment and improvement of the methodology (recording, sampling, processing).

The combination of the two models of depth (Fig. 5.5) and the potential existence of antiquities (Fig. 5.4) is useful to be able to determine the depth of excavation without being so concerned about the discovery of antiquities, if someone wants to build outside a potentially archaeological surface. The same is also true for potential archaeological surfaces, where the non-existence of antiquities in a specific locality is not sufficient to reassure investors, who must always be prepared for any eventuality. However, this interests mainly the municipal authorities which are involved, the

City Planning Department and the City Council, which lay down the building regulations and issue planning permission, and ought in principle to protect citizens.

The final result of the processing of the two models is depicted on the map in Figure 5.8.

The attempt to compare the map in Figure 5.8 with known archaeological data is not technically feasible. Usually, in archaeological studies which do not constitute specialised publications of archaeological research little information about depths is provided. Thus, there is no yardstick immediately available since on the few occasions on which a rescue excavation is published, the information provided about the depths does not always concern the deposition which separates the archaeological layer from the surface of the ground, but focuses mainly on the dimensions and positions of the finds within the archaeological layer. However, studying some details on the maps leads to interesting observations.

The sites with the shallower known depth of non-archaeological deposits are principally located in the area to the south of the castle (Fig. 5.8: no. 1) as well as Pagona (Fig. 5.8: no. 2), where a prehistoric settlement has been discovered. The deposition is between 0.8 and 1.5m thick, and then follows the archaeological layer.

Such a shallow depth does not always mean the existence of antiquities close to the surface. In some cases it simply characterises the intention of builders not to lay foundations at great depths, whether they want to avoid antiquities or for other reasons.

Shallow depths are predicted around known or potential archaeological sites, e.g.:

1. around a Roman farmhouse (Fig. 5.8: no. 3), [1.1-1.4m],
2. at Pagona (Fig. 5.8: no. 2), where there is a Roman road [1-1.4m] and a prehistoric settlement [0.8-1.3m],
3. west of the northern cemetery (Fig. 5.8: no. 4) [1.2-1.5m],
4. south of the northwestern cemetery (Fig. 5.8: no. 5) [1.2-1.4m],
5. around the castle and within the ancient urban area (Fig. 5.8: no. 1) [1.1-1.5m].

The areas with a predicted maximum known depth of non-archaeological deposits of 1.5 to 2.5m occupy by far the biggest part of the City Plan, but with a limited surface of potential archaeological sites and their surrounding areas. These include prehistoric sites (Fig. 5.8: no. 6) [1.8-1.9m], and Roman sites, like roads, (Fig. 5.8: no. 7) [1.6-3.2m], burial sites (Fig. 5.8: no. 8, 9) [1.4-2.2m], (Fig. 5.8: no. 5) [2.2-2.7m], the ancient port (Fig. 5.8: no. 10) [1.7-2.4m], and others (Fig. 5.8: no. 11) [1.6-2.4m], (Fig. 5.8: no. 12) [2.2-2.7m].

A very small part of the surface has a predicted maximum known depth of non-archaeological deposits of 2.5m and over. In this zone there is very little potential for the existence of archaeological sites, not because the archaeological depths do not extend so far down, but because their horizons are usually at a shallower depth (Fig. 5.8: no. 13 [up to 2.9m], no. 7 [up to 3.2m), no. 14 [2.2-2.7m].

5.3.3 Conclusion

An analytical presentation has been made of the procedure followed for choosing potential predictors among the available variables from the excavational data so as to create a predictive model. This procedure resulted in the exclusion of two variables and the employment of the only one which was deemed suitable. The final step was to combine this predictive model which depicts the potential maximum known depth of non-archaeological deposits with the model of potential archaeological sites, which had been constructed earlier using the Thiessen polygons technique. In this way a unified predictive model was generated, which predicts the depth of detection of the archaeological horizon only in those areas of the city which constitute the potential archaeological sites of the city.

The permanent effectiveness and usefulness of this final model will be achieved through the continuous enrichment of the database with new information, but also with new parameters, which may highlight other dimensions of the topic. This depends to a great extent on how analytical and detailed the description of excavational data is, but also how and whether the ever-developing technology is utilised to the full.

5.4 Archaeological excavations and the building regulations of the city

The discovery of antiquities during excavations is an event which directly affects the course of a construction project. At this point the reverse process will be explored, that is, to what extent the conditions and regulations associated with a construction project affect the discovery and subsequent fate of antiquities. This knowledge, in combination with the ability to predict potential archaeological sites in specific locations and at specific depths in the city, can prove exceptionally useful for the promotion of archaeological research and generally for the management of the underground cultural heritage of a contemporary historical city. Furthermore, the procedure of city planning is enhanced with the appropriate adaptation of its building regulations, mainly the floor area ratio, based on the presence of antiquities within and under the contemporary urban fabric.

The questions which were posed can be summarised as follows:

1. Is the distribution of archaeological excavations in the city uniform in relation to the total number of the excavations?
2. How does the distribution of archaeological sites on both buildable and unbuildable land differ in terms of the type, chronology and preservation status of antiquities?

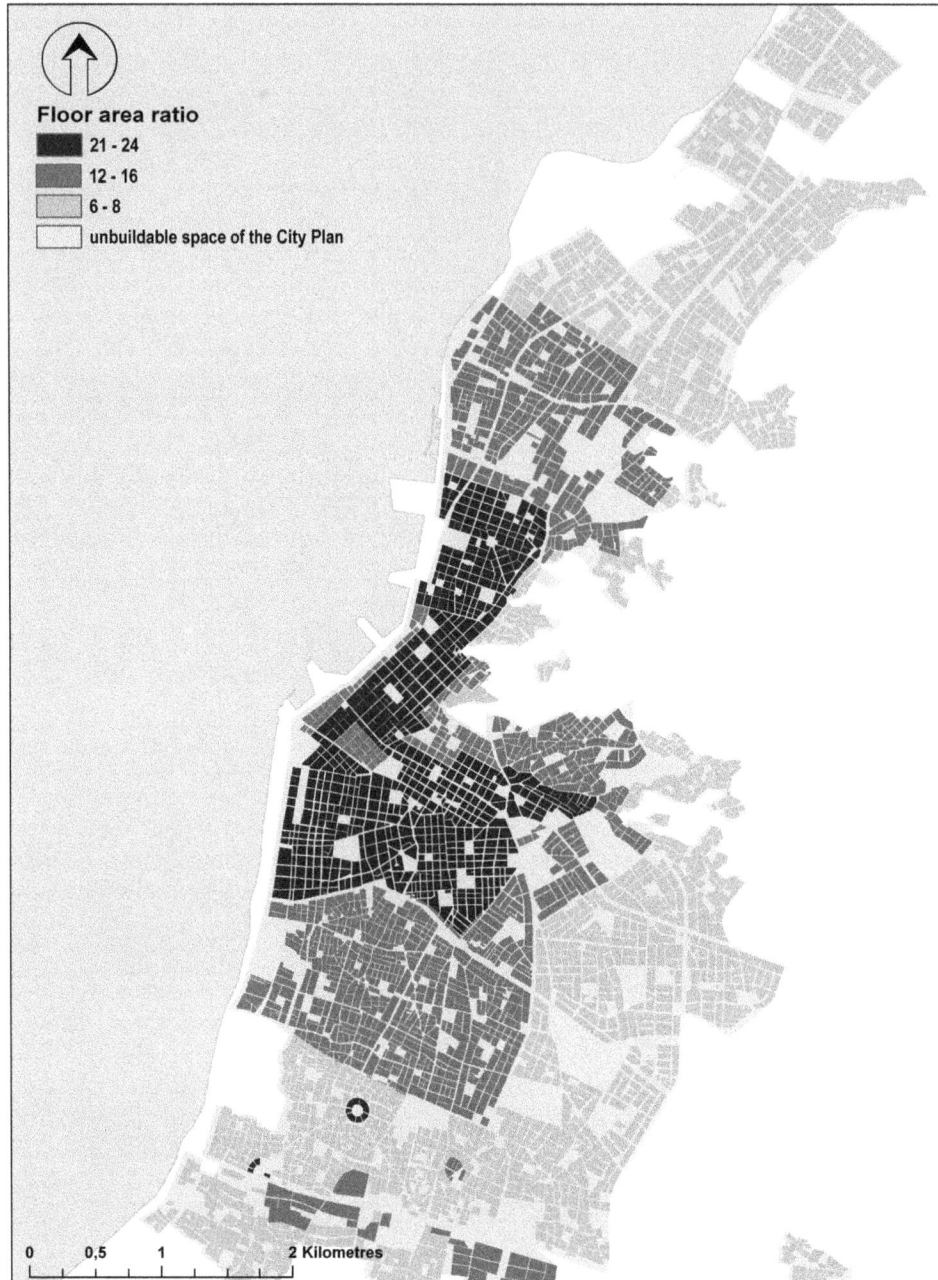

Fig. 5.9: The distribution of zones of f.a.r. in the City Plan of Patras (Source: Base Map: Laboratory of Urban and Regional Planning – University of Patras, Map Composition: the author).

3. In which zones of the buildable and unbuildable surface of the city are there more potential archaeological sites?
4. Is the distribution of the maximum known depths of non-archaeological deposits uniform or does it differ in the buildable and unbuildable areas and how is that depth related to the intended depth of excavation in the same locations?

These questions were explored with a series of statistical tests. Apart from answering these questions, a statistical test was also run on the distribution of delay in working days from the start of the rescue excavation until the completion of archaeological research. The test did not yield statistically significant results due to the inadequate recording of the required data.

5.4.1 Classification of the building regulations into groups and the calculation of the surface of the City Plan

The city planning regulations which were used were the floor area ratio (f.a.r.), which is considered to be the most important regulation, the maximum permitted height (m.p.h.) and maximum permitted coverage (m.p.c.).

The values of the f.a.r were classified according to the 'natural break' method, a method which presents the data distribution in a better way (Conolly & Lake, 2006: 142). Three groups were formed: the low (values: 0.6-0.8), the medium (values: 1.2-1.6) and the high (values: 2.1-2.4) (Fig. 5.9).

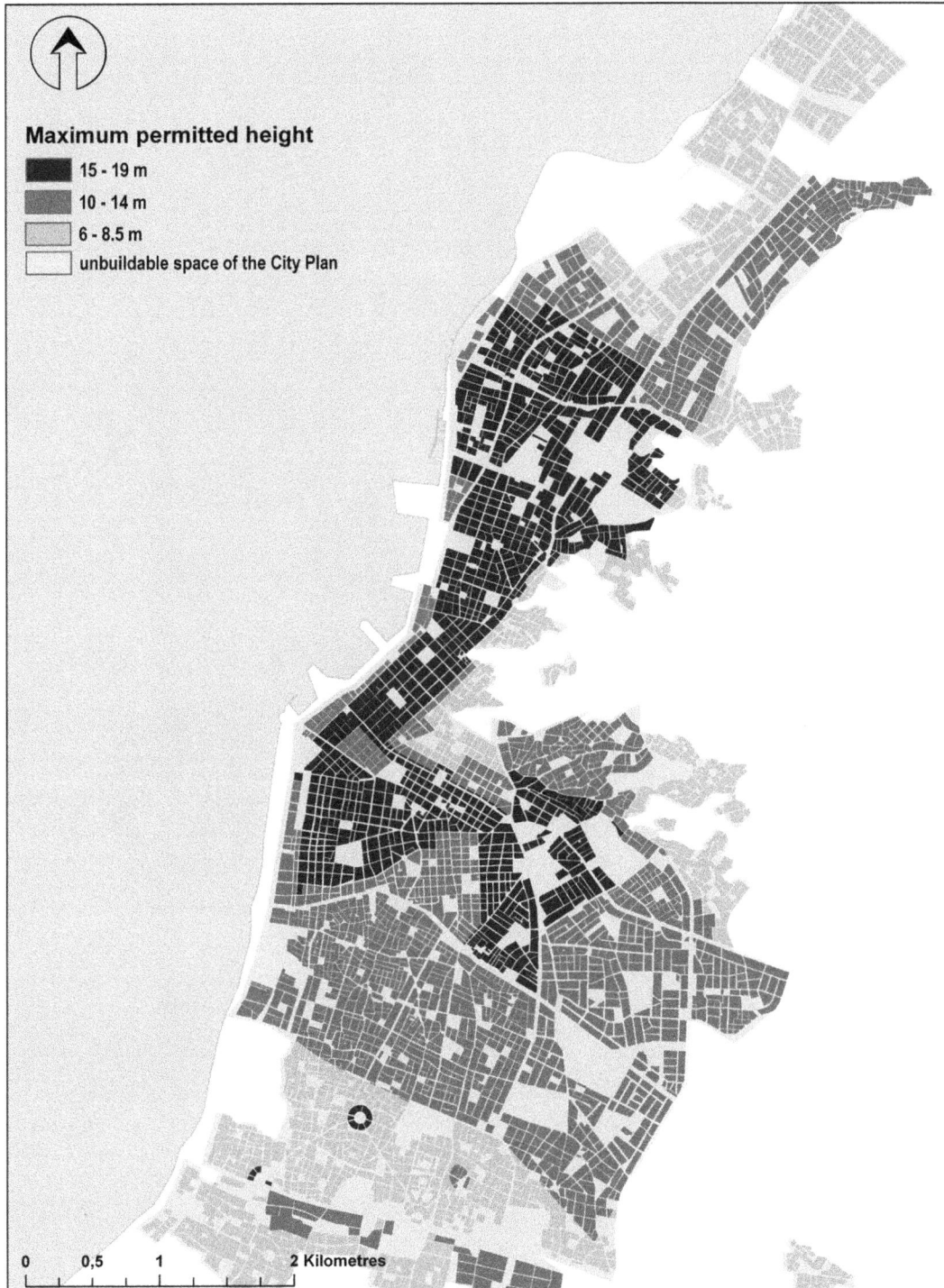

Fig. 5.10: The distribution of zones of m.p.h. in the City Plan of Patras (Source: Base Map: Laboratory of Urban and Regional Planning – University of Patras, Map Composition: the author).

Likewise, the values for the m.p.h. were classified into groups: the low (values: 6-8.5m), the medium (values: 10-14m) and the high (values: 16-19m) (Fig. 5.10).

Furthermore, another group was added, that of public spaces, which are not governed by planning regulations since they form an unbuildable surface of the City Plan. The classification of the regulations into groups was judged worthwhile in order to avoid the confusion which a large amount of data would cause for the execution of statistical

tests and to gain a better picture of the contribution of building regulations to the detection of antiquities and further management of archaeological excavations.

As far as the regulation 'maximum permitted coverage' is concerned, it was not deemed worthwhile to classify the cases into groups, since 82% of the excavations within the buildable surface had a maximum permitted coverage of 70%. Thus, the test finally concerned two distinct zones, the buildable and unbuildable. The surface

Table 5.12: Observed and expected number of archaeological excavations in the buildable and unbuildable space, based on the surface of each zone.

CITY ZONES	Observed number of archaeolog. excavations	Expected number of archaeolog. excavations	CELL COUNT
Buildable	90	123	20,405
Unbuildable	57	24	3,961
TOTAL	147	147	24,366

of the City Plan was calculated using GIS. The thematic database was georeferenced to the digital map of the City Plan of Patras. The existing vector structure of the map was rasterised.

In this way, the study area was divided into a series of distinct spatial units of the same size, the cells, which form the total area, in the same way that a mosaic consists of separate tiles. In each cell is stored data which represents the properties of the object which it describes as well as its geographical coordinates. It is, in other words, stored data which concerns the geographical space which it represents (Pappas, 2011: 132-133; Kvamme, 1990b: 370-371). In order for the buildable zone surface and the public space to be measured, the cells that are located in those zones were counted. The total surface represents the sum of the cells in the two zones.

In order for the uniformity of the distribution to be tested, an expected value was calculated based on a theoretical hypothesis. For example, if it is considered that the archaeological sites are distributed uniformly in both of the zones of the City Plan, then the buildable zone, which represents 84% of the surface (or 20,405 cells), will represent 84% (123) of the archaeological excavations. In the unbuildable zone, which represents 16% of the surface (or 3,962 cells), 24 archaeological excavations will be found, that is, 16% of the total count (Table 5.12).

The hypothesis applies if the Null Hypothesis is true, that there is no difference between the distribution of archaeological excavations in the two zones, in proportion to the size of each surface.

5.4.2 Distribution of the excavations

Null Hypothesis: there is no difference in the distribution of excavations in the city, whether they are in the buildable or unbuildable area, as well as the different zones of the buildable surface. The x^2 statistical test was run (see Appendix: Tables 1 & 2).

Within the City Plan 84% is taken up by buildable space, that is, building plots, and 16% constitutes unbuildable space, that is, public spaces, facilities and the road network (Fig. 5.11).

If the surface of the city is considered to be divided into these two basic planning zones, it can be ascertained that during the period which is being studied, despite the fact that the distribution of excavations is not uniform in

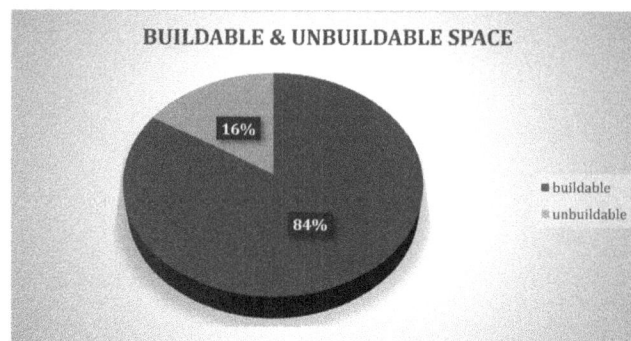

Fig. 5.11: Distribution of buildable and unbuildable space in Patras.

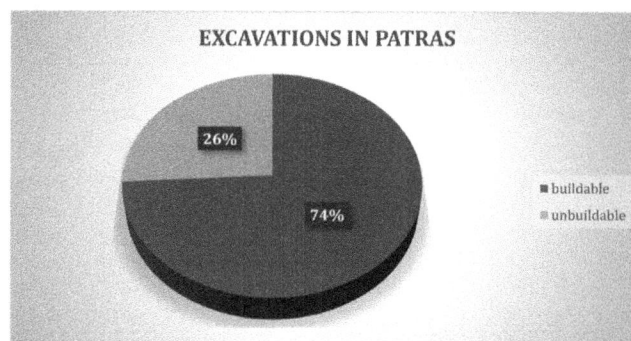

Fig. 5.12: Distribution of excavations in the buildable and unbuildable space of the City Plan.

proportion to the surface of the space, in absolute numbers there are three times more excavations in the buildable zone than in the unbuildable one. 58.5% more excavations were carried out in public spaces and 11% fewer in the buildable zone than would be expected in a uniform distribution (see Appendix: Table 1 & Fig. 5.12).

However, within the buildable zone fewer excavations were conducted in areas with a low (-48%) and medium (-21%) f.a.r and many more in sites with a high ratio (+121%) than would be expected in a uniform distribution (see Appendix: Table 2 & Fig. 5.13 and 5.14).

The cause of this differentiation is probably due to the fact that in the areas with a high f.a.r. there are more fragmented plots, whereas in the other zones the plots are larger.

5.4.3 Distribution of the archaeological excavations

Null Hypothesis: there is no difference in the distribution of archaeological excavations in the city, whether they are in the buildable or unbuildable area, as well as the different zones of the buildable surface, and the distribution is

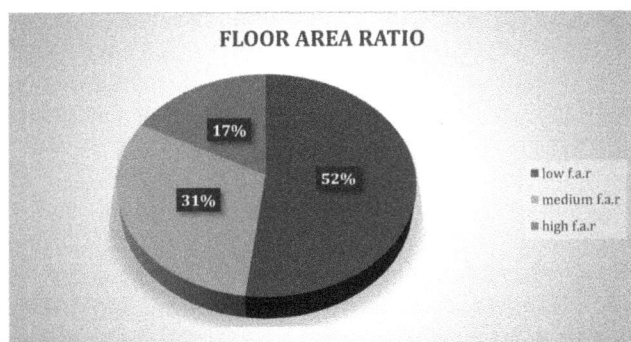

Fig. 5.13: The distribution of f.a.r. in Patras.

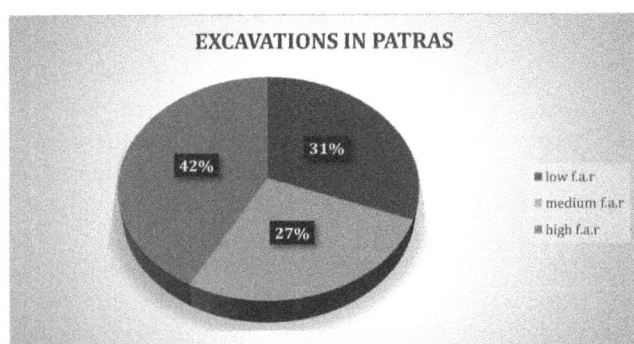

Fig. 5.14: The distribution of excavations in the buildable space of the City Plan according to the f.a.r.

uniform and proportional to the size of the examined zone. The x^2 statistical test was run (see Appendix: Tables 3 & 4).

At first sight, the archaeological excavations show a similar distribution in the city to that of all the excavations, whether archaeological or not, in other words, fewer than expected in the buildable zone and more in the unbuildable zone (Fig. 5.15).

However, even though the excavations are fewer than expected (-11%), the archaeological excavations are even fewer (-26.5%). On the other hand, the discrepancy between the total number of excavations (58.5%) and the archaeological ones in particular (50%) in the unbuildable zone is very small, which means that the distribution of archaeological excavations in the public space is proportional to the excavational works which take place in those areas (see Appendix: Table 3).

Within the buildable surface the archaeological excavations are fewer in number and in proportion regarding their surface in the low and medium zones (-78.2% and -47.6% respectively) but more numerous (+172.5%) in the high zone (see Appendix: Table 4 & Fig. 5.16). Following the rationale that was developed in the distribution of excavations, it appears that the reason that was mentioned above applies, that is, the area with high f.a.r. has denser and more fragmented plots, while the other zones have larger plots.

In general, from the statistical tests it can be seen that antiquities are more frequently located in the unbuildable zone, but also in the zone with high f.a.r. Perhaps the

antiquities tend to be located in public and commercially unexploitable land or on private property consisting of fragmented spaces where they cannot remain hidden.

5.4.4 Distribution of chronological periods

Null Hypothesis: there is no difference in the distribution of historical periods as they are represented in the rescue excavations, whether in the buildable or unbuildable area, as well as in the different zones of the buildable surface, and the distribution is uniform and proportional to the size of the examined zone. The x^2 statistical test was run (see Appendix: Tables 5 – 7).

Prior to any form of analysis, it must be stressed that the dating of archaeological sites at this stage of the study is not final. It is based on a first diagnosis of the finds by the researchers and is subject to chronological shifts which only become known with the excavators' final publication. Consequently, finds which belong chronologically to transitional phases may have been dated to a particular period, whereas they actually belong to a later or earlier one. For that reason, the chronology is broadly divided into Prehistoric, Classical/Hellenistic, Roman, Byzantine and Post-Byzantine (see Appendix: Table 5).

The Prehistoric finds are located in a buildable zone with a low f.a.r. and m.p.h.. Usually, these planning regulations are associated with a shallower depth of excavation and, by extension, less interference with the antiquities which may be found below. In addition, the low height of buildings adjacent to potential archaeological sites is

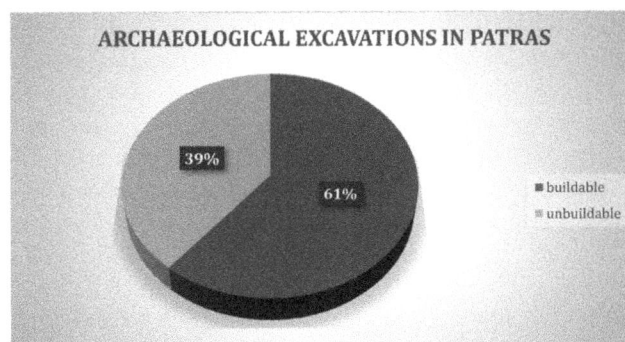

Fig. 5.15: The distribution of archaeological excavations in the buildable and unbuildable space of the City Plan.

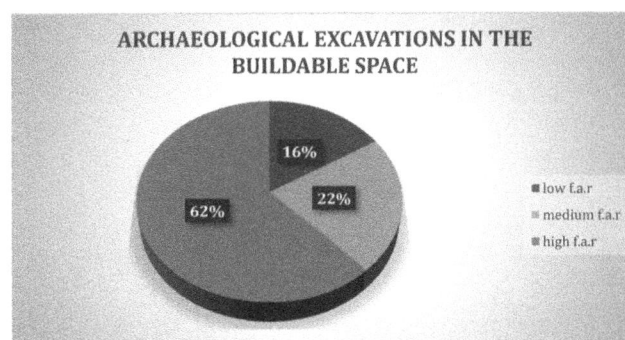

Fig. 5.16: The distribution of archaeological excavations in the buildable space of the City Plan according to the f.a.r.

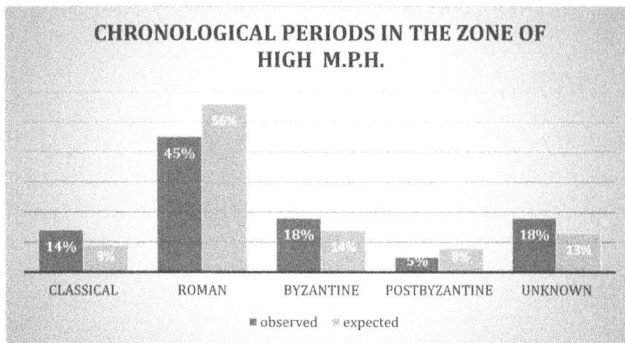

CHRONOLOGICAL PERIODS IN THE ZONE OF HIGH M.P.H.

Fig. 5.17: Distribution of chronological periods in the excavations within the zone of high m.p.h. in Patras.

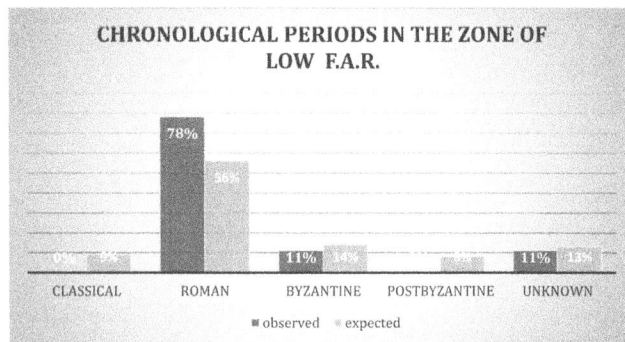

CHRONOLOGICAL PERIODS IN THE ZONE OF LOW F.A.R.

Fig. 5.18: Distribution of chronological periods in the excavations within the zone of low f.a.r. in Patras.

conducive to the future preservation of the antiquities and its transformation into a space open to the public, since the absence of high buildings does not reduce the visibility of the site.

On the other hand, the classical antiquities, which do not have a uniform distribution in the space either, are mostly located in the zone of high m.p.h. in the most densely populated part of the city, causing further pressure with their great heights and great depths of foundations on the finds which are conjectured to be below plots, thus making it more difficult to salvage and display them (see Appendix: Table 6 & Fig. 5.17).

As far as the other chronological periods are concerned, the Null Hypothesis regarding uniform distribution in the zone of high f.a.r. cannot be disproved, something though which is the case in the zones of low and medium f.a.r. (see Appendix: Table 7 & Fig. 5.18 and 5.19).

As can be seen in Table 5 of the Appendix, antiquities which date from the Roman period are not only not distributed uniformly, but are also mostly located in the unbuildable surface and particularly in the modern road network (Fig. 5.20).

The Roman antiquities of this zone are related to the remains of the road and water supply networks, two types of infrastructure which reached their peak during the Roman period and remained in use for many centuries after the collapse of the Roman empire, even until the 19th century. Indeed, older excavations revealed that the modern

road network to a large extent follows the ancient one. In addition, it is relatively common for an archaeological layer to have been destroyed under a road which has been used throughout time, in contrast to what happens at an inhabited site.

This, however, results in the representation of this period in Patras lacking typological variety in proportion to the surface which the contemporary city covers. Nevertheless, it is this typological variety, however limited, which casts light on different aspects of public and private life in each period. Particular types of finds e.g. remains of housing, movable finds, etc., better characterise their time, constitute expressions of short-lived tendencies and fashion and can therefore be dated more accurately.

As far as the buildable surface is concerned, a wider variety of chronological periods could be discovered, but since many Classical, Byzantine and Post-Byzantine sites are located in areas with medium or high building regulations, the chances of protecting and displaying them are reduced by their proximity to buildings up to 19m high. Nevertheless, these sites, with the appropriate management, could become the necessary open spaces that a densely populated urban area requires.

5.4.5 Distribution of typology

Null Hypothesis: there is no difference in the distribution of the typology of the finds which were discovered at the rescue excavations, whether in the buildable or unbuildable area, as well as in the different zones of the buildable

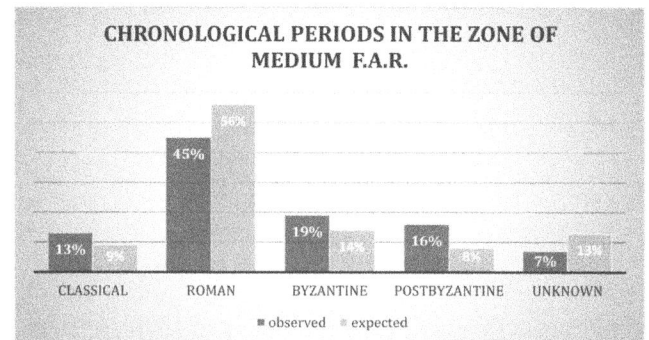

CHRONOLOGICAL PERIODS IN THE ZONE OF MEDIUM F.A.R.

Fig. 5.19: Distribution of chronological periods in the excavations within the zone of medium f.a.r. in Patras.

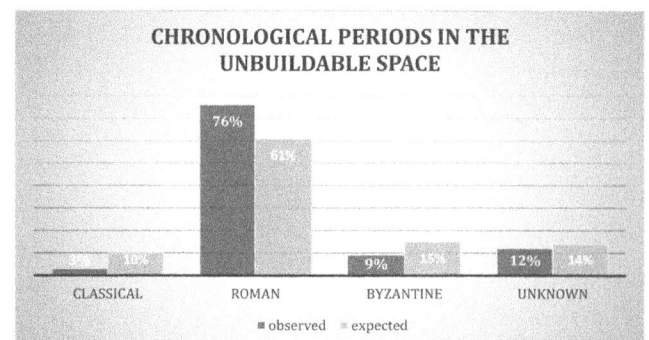

CHRONOLOGICAL PERIODS IN THE UNBUILDABLE SPACE

Fig. 5.20: Distribution of chronological periods in the excavations within the unbuildable zone in Patras.

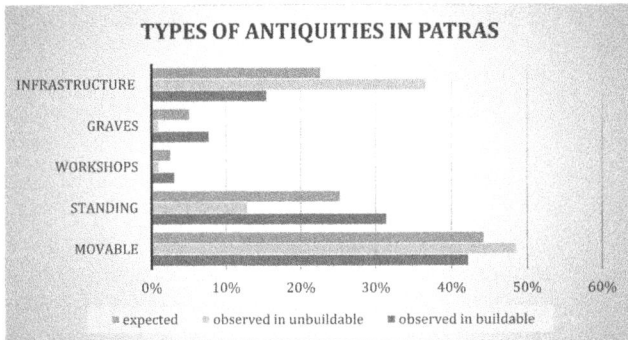

Fig. 5.21: Distribution of typology of antiquities at the rescue excavations in Patras.

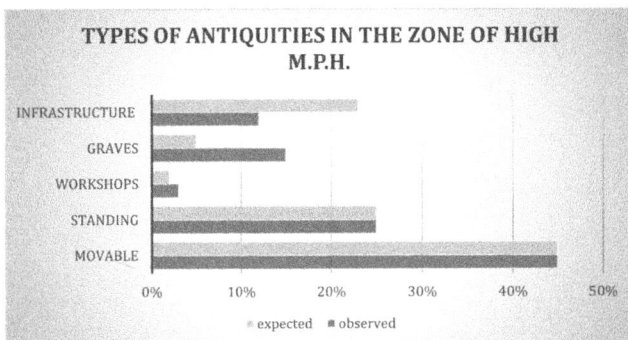

Fig. 5.22: Distribution of typology of antiquities at the rescue excavations within the zone of high m.p.h. in Patras.

surface and the distribution is uniform and proportional to the size of the examined zone. The x^2 statistical test was run (see Appendix: Tables 8 & 9).

It has already been established that the typological representation of the antiquities differs between the buildable and unbuildable zones. More than half of the infrastructural networks (roads, water supply) are found in the unbuildable zone of the public spaces. On the other hand, more remains of residences, public buildings, workshops and cemeteries are discovered on the buildable surface (see Appendix: Table 8 & Fig. 5.21).

In the zone of high m.p.h. there are mostly finds from burial sites (Fig. 5.22 & Appendix: Table 9). Two thirds of the graves have been discovered in this area, which coincides with the northern cemetery, the southwestern cemetery and part of the southeastern one. It is quite common for parts of the ancient cemeteries found in older rescue excavations to be preserved in the basements of blocks of flats.

However, it is obvious that the planning of basements is rather problematic due to the serious likelihood of there being antiquities. Furthermore, managing antiquities in this area is extremely difficult because the existence of buildings up to 19m high around an archaeological site blocks the view of and access to the monument, unless an open protection zone around it has been allowed for. However, this is almost impossible in the zone with the greatest density of habitation and land use, while the expropriation of many adjacent plots of land would have

an unbearable economic and social cost for the city and the Archaeological Service.

Nevertheless, from an archaeological perspective, the burial sites provide some of the most impressive and enlightening finds due to their abundance, as well as their artistic, historical, religious and material importance.

5.4.6 Distribution of the preservation status of the excavated sites

Null Hypothesis: there is no difference in the distribution of the types of preservation status of the rescue excavations, whether in the buildable or unbuildable area, as well as in the different zones of the buildable surface, and the distribution is uniform and proportional to the size of the examined area. The x^2 statistical test was run (see Appendix: Tables 10 & 11).

The test yields interesting results. Since no site was considered worth preserving and being made visible and open to the public, there were two principal options, that is, the reburial of immovable building remains or their demolition.

Almost half the reburials take place in the unbuildable zone (Fig. 5.23) which occupies just 17% of the total surface. This practice is considered to be the most advisable for the preservation of archaeological heritage. In 63% of the cases in this zone, the antiquities are reburied, which does not happen in the buildable zone.

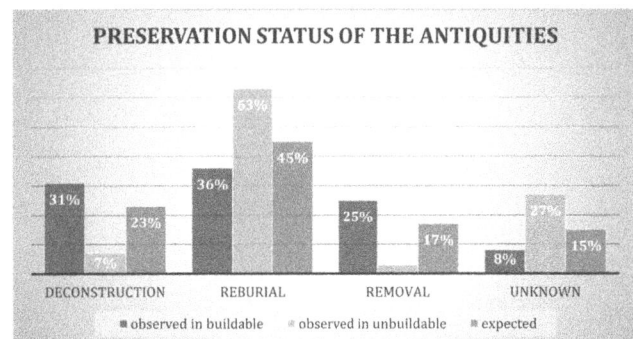

Fig. 5.23: Distribution of the type of preservation status of the rescue excavations in Patras.

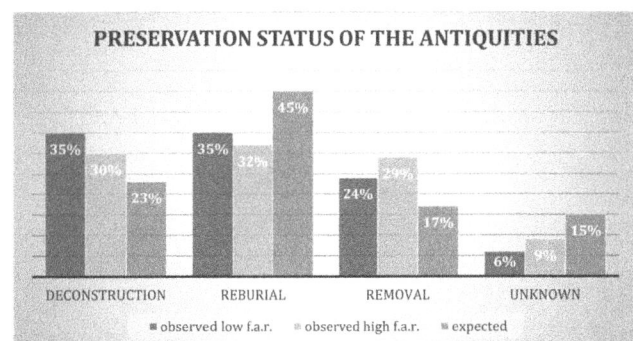

Fig. 5.24: Distribution of the type of preservation status of the rescue excavations within the zones of low and high f.a.r. in Patras.

In contrast, 9 out of 10 demolitions take place in the buildable zone. Not only is the distribution of sites which are destroyed in this way not uniform, but it also appears that 36.6% more demolitions take place (see Appendix: Table 11). This represents statistical proof that, due to a lack of funds available for the compensation of owners, demolition is preferred on private land (Fig. 5.24).

In conclusion, there is a statistically significant dependence of the types of preservation status on the buildable surfaces. With the exception of the zone of medium f.a.r., where the distribution of the types of preservation status is uniform, a different picture appears in the other buildable zones. There, the adoption of a 'destructive' method prevails and a more protective method, such as reburial, gradually gives ground as the f.a.r. increases in the buildable part of the city.

5.4.7 Distribution of potential archaeological surface

Null Hypothesis: there is no difference in the distribution of the potential archaeological surface in the city, whether in the buildable or unbuildable area, as well as in the different zones of the buildable surface, and the distribution is uniform and proportional to the size of the examined zone. The x^2 statistical test was run (see Appendix: Tables 12 & 13).

Comparing the potential archaeological surface in the buildable and unbuildable areas of the city, it can be seen that in the latter it is conjectured that fewer (around 24%) archaeological sites would be discovered than those expected in a uniform distribution (Fig. 5.25, see Appendix: Table 12).

As far as the buildable space is concerned (Fig. 5.25, see Appendix: Table 13), it appears that in areas with a high f.a.r. the potential archaeological surface leaps to 205% of that expected in a uniform distribution. In this way, a statistically significant indication is provided of where archaeological research is likely to concentrate its efforts in the future and, as a consequence, in which areas special action will have to be taken in the context of city planning in order to protect both antiquities and investors.

5.4.8 Distribution of intended excavation depths

Null Hypothesis: there is no difference in the distribution of intended excavation depths in the city, whether in the buildable or unbuildable areas, as well as in the different zones of the buildable surface, and the samples in all the zones have the same median value of excavation depth. The Mann Whitney U-test and Kruskall-Wallis statistical tests were run (see Appendix: Tables 14-18).

The examination of all the intended excavation depths of all the sites in the study in the buildable or unbuildable areas does not yield statistically significant results. This means that the median depths of the two groups do not differ very much, so that the difference is not statistically significant (see Appendix: Table 14). However, a separate examination of this relationship for archaeological and non-archaeological excavations yields statistically significant results which can be subjected to further interpretation.

In relation to the archaeological excavations, the Null Hypothesis is disproved. The median value is 2.5m for the buildable zone and just 0.8m for public land, whereas the difference between their mean values is also obvious (Fig. 5.26, see Appendix: Table 15). As far as the non-archaeological excavations are concerned, in neither case is the Null Hypothesis true and the public space has higher median and mean intended excavation depths, something which obviously does not present any obstacle as no antiquities are detected (Fig. 5.26, see Appendix: Table 16).

A thorough examination of the buildable zone reveals that both the median and mean values for the archaeological excavations rise gradually with the increase in the f.a.r. (Fig. 5.27, see Appendix: Tables 17 & 18). As a result, archaeological sites located in areas with a high f.a.r. have a better chance of being discovered and their layers risk being disturbed to a greater extent.

This phenomenon can be seen in reverse. The stakeholders in areas of high f.a.r. are totally unprepared for or ignorant of the risk of encountering antiquities and of being forced to interrupt their work in order for rescue research to be carried out. However, there is no corresponding relationship between the planning regulations and the

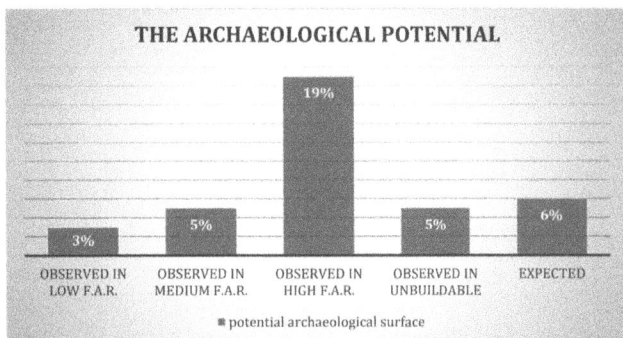

Fig. 5.25: Distribution of the potential archaeological surface in Patras.

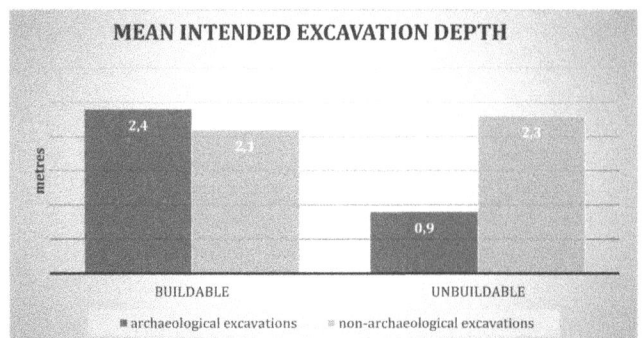

Fig. 5.26: Mean intended excavation depth throughout the City Plan area.

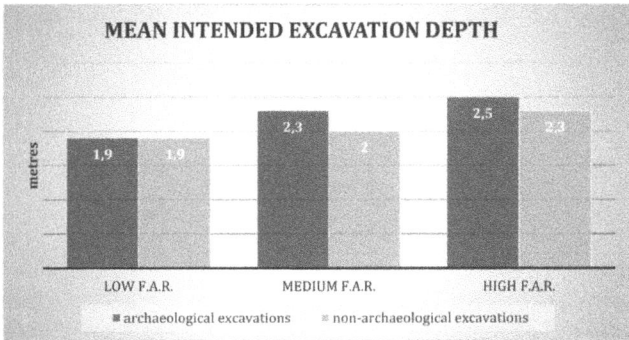

Fig. 5.27: Mean intended excavation depth in the buildable space of the City Plan.

potential existence of archaeological layers. As a result, the intended excavation depths in the areas with high building regulations coincide to a great extent with the archaeological surface.

5.4.9 Distribution of maximum known depth without archaeological deposits

Null Hypothesis: there is no difference in the distribution of maximum known depth without archaeological deposits in the city, whether in the buildable or unbuildable areas, as well as in the different zones of the buildable surface, and the samples in all the zones have the same median value of maximum known depth without archaeological deposits. The Mann Whitney U-test and Kruskall-Wallis statistical tests were run (see Appendix: Tables 19-22).

Comparing only the values for the archaeological excavations in both tests, the Null Hypothesis cannot be true (see Appendix: Tables 19 & 20). A difference of roughly half a metre can be observed between the median value in the buildable and unbuildable zones. More specifically, in the unbuildable area the smallest median and mean values of depth without archaeological deposits are present (Fig. 5.28), whereas in the buildable zones the corresponding figures exceed a depth of 1m (Fig. 5.29).

Based on the values of the non-archaeological excavations in both tests, the Null Hypothesis is disproved (see Appendix: Tables 21 & 22). The median and mean values in the public spaces zone are found to be lower than in the buildable zone (Fig. 5.28).

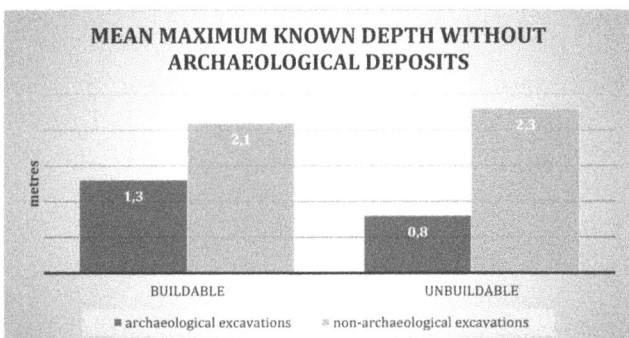

Fig. 5.28: Mean maximum known depth without archaeological deposits at the excavations in Patras.

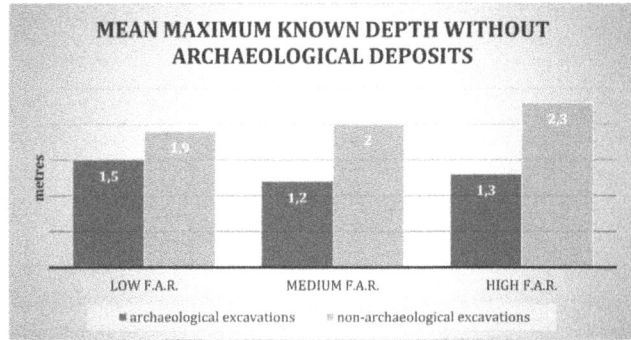

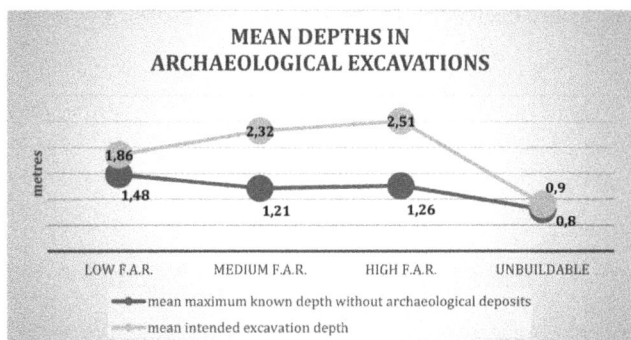

Fig. 5.29: Mean maximum known depth without archaeological deposits at the excavations within the buildable space of Patras.

Within the buildable zone, the higher the f.a.r. is, the greater the mean value of depth is, particularly in the area with a high f.a.r., where it reaches 2.3m for a total of 234 excavations, whereas the median is 2.5m (Fig. 5.29).

In order for these differences to become more easily understood, there follows a comparison of the mean values of the two variables which have just been examined, in other words, of the mean 'intended excavation depth' and of the mean 'maximum known depth without archaeological deposits' (Fig. 5.30 & 5.31).

In this way, the level of awareness of and preparedness for the possibility of encountering antiquities hidden below the

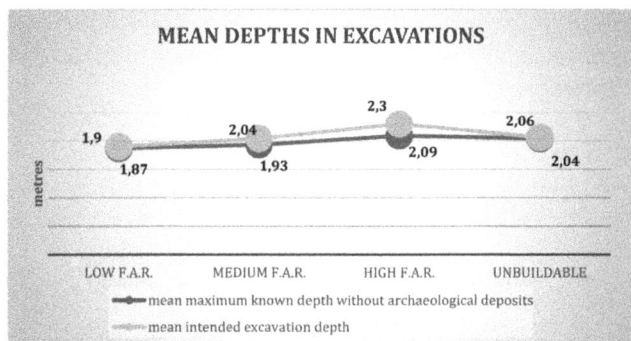

Fig. 5.30: Mean intended depth of excavation and mean maximum known depth without archaeological deposits at the excavations in Patras.

Fig. 5.31: Mean intended excavation depth and mean maximum known depth without archaeological deposits at the archaeological excavations in Patras.

ground which characterises city planning in every surface of the City Plan of Patras can be demonstrated.

In the zone with a low f.a.r. ground disturbance of 40cm is expected, whereas in the zones with a medium and high f.a.r. the disturbance of the archaeological layer ranges from 1.10m to 1.20m. What is ironic, though, is what can be seen in the non-archaeological excavations in the buildable zones. The mean and median intended excavation depths are shallower than the corresponding figures for archaeological excavations, whereas the opposite would be expected, with better informed and more wary stakeholders (see Appendix: Tables 17 & 18). The zone which is most conducive to the management of existing antiquities is that of the public spaces, where, since the two variables of depth occasionally coincide or are very close, the archaeological layer is subject to little or no disturbance when it is discovered.

5.4.10 Conclusion

The series of statistical tests that were performed demonstrated that the distribution of archaeological excavations in the city is not uniform and that the possibility of discovering antiquities during construction projects is very much influenced by the location, namely, whether a project takes place in public space or on privately owned plots with a high or low f.a.r.

Even when archaeological sites come to light, there is a bias in their typological and chronological characteristics, favouring certain periods and types of finds, such as Prehistoric habitation sites and Roman roads at the expense of others, such as Classical cemeteries. Likewise, the chances of the recovered antiquities being preserved after the completion of archaeological investigations are not equal throughout the city. The most desirable type of preservation, the reburial, is practised more often in public space, while the catastrophic practice of demolition is exercised in the buildable zones of the city.

Furthermore, the distribution of intended excavation depth is not uniform, either. The archaeological excavations have a greater excavation depth than the non- archaeological ones. Thus, the archaeological palimpsest is put under greater pressure and risk, while the landowners concerned are obliged to modify their plans and increase their budgets.

Under these conditions, the distribution of potential archaeological zones assumes great importance. According to predictive modelling, future archaeological research will focus more on the buildable zones rather than on public spaces. There more than anywhere else will it be necessary for those involved in works to cooperate with each other, and to test how adaptable the expected cultural resources are to the development plan and how easy they are to manage. In the light of this data, the introduction of a new building regulation is proposed.

Chapter 6

General Conclusion and Future Prospects

6.1 Results, Discussion and a New Building Regulation

The idea that the archaeological potential of a modern yet historical city can be explored with the use of predictive modelling was put forward in the previous chapters of the book. The reason was that, if no steps are taken, modern construction projects will constitute a threat for the rich archaeological palimpsest and vice versa. The discovery of antiquities and the archaeological research that follows will delay or cancel the construction.

From what has been written thus far, it is clear that archaeological research needs to be approached as part of the city planning/construction procedure with the development of the methodology in order to improve cooperation between the partners involved in the statutory stages of planning. The incorporation of urban archaeological research into the general planning procedure represents a realistic proposition which can be implemented within the existing institutional environment, by creating a model of cooperation and management for the city planning procedure and archaeological research.

Since the research questions (see chapter 1) had never been discussed from this particular perspective before, their investigation involved the use of methods derived from landscape archaeology, but with a pioneering approach, the utilisation of available sources of information which to date have not been studied, such as excavations, and the use of interdisciplinary applications within existing institutional frameworks. The city of Patras was selected for the case study and, more specifically, the area included in the City Plan.

Landscape archaeology provided the conceptual definition of space as consisting of sites and non-sites, with characteristics which can be analysed quantitatively and spatially. The excavation reports proved to be a very revealing though thus far neglected source of information about the relationship between construction projects and archaeological resources. Finally, the interdisciplinary approach allowed the integration of arguments and techniques from different disciplines into one unified study. Besides, it was very much encouraged by the opinions of various experts and practitioners of spatial planning and cultural management in Patras, who were interviewed, and considered the lack of interdisciplinarity as a major obstacle in their work.

Using a combination of methods of spatial analysis and statistical processing, the existing knowledge in those fields was examined and assessed. Several GIS techniques were employed and new information was generated in the form of predictive models and distribution patterns.

In addition, the connection between the information from excavations/rescue excavations and building regulations, particularly the floor area ratio and, of secondary importance, the maximum permitted height and the maximum permitted coverage, was examined with a series of statistical tests, both parametric and non-parametric.

As a result, a series of maps was produced depicting potential archaeological surfaces all over Patras and the depth at which archaeological resources are expected to be found in every locality of this surface. One of these maps (see Fig. 5.8) can serve as a model of potential archaeological sites and potential minimum depth of discovery of the archaeological layer within the City Plan of Patras.

A model based on the proposed methodology can be evaluated by comparing it with other models which use GIS technology, by using some other equivalent technology based on modern techniques of spatial analysis or by using the empirical observations of archaeologists regarding the topography of the ancient city. In practice, the first alternative is not feasible, because GIS applications in urban archaeology are not widespread and there has certainly never been such a specialised study of this type for Patras. This is an unexplored field, which in the future merits attention from other scholars and represents the starting point for a constructive debate and the promotion of methods of urban archaeology. Therefore, for the time being, evaluation could only be carried out using the validation methods provided by GIS and the empirical findings of practitioners in the city.

Based on empirical observation it appeared that the potential archaeological surface of the model coincides with the published archaeological map of the city (Fig. 4.2), which is based on the research of the Archaeological Service. The difference is that the model is derived from data from a five-year-period, whereas the archaeological map is derived from data from all the investigations which took place up to the beginning of the 21st c. A corresponding comparison of empirical findings with the model of potential maximum known depth without archaeological deposits cannot be made because an equivalent archaeological map does not exist. Usually, in archaeological studies which do not involve a specialised publication of an excavation depths are not mentioned. As a result, there is no immediate yardstick, since on the few occasions on which a rescue excavation is published, the information provided about depths is not connected with the deposition which separates the horizon of the archaeological layer from the surface of the ground but with the dimensions and positions of finds within the archaeological layer.

Validation in a GIS environment is a quantitative procedure that calculates the prediction error. Programmers set certain criteria so that a user is in a position to judge objectively the degree to which the model gives accurate estimates. Prediction error can be further tested by using descriptive statistics which show the distribution of error both on the whole surface and locally and also take into consideration the specific characteristics of each case separately. In our case, the error distribution is close to normal. The mean value is 0.05m and the median value is 0.1m. Of the 138 archaeological excavations, 90 sites (65%) are found at a depth with a difference of half a metre from that estimated. It is worth noting that in all of the applications, each time that more data was added to the dataset, all the predictions improved, with a corresponding decrease in prediction error.

The statistical tests that followed gave new insights, too. The distribution of archaeological excavations within the City Plan area is not only not uniform in relation to the total number of excavations in the same area, but there are also fewer archaeological excavations in the zones of low and medium f.a.r. and more in the zone of high f.a.r. and in the public spaces. Thus, it seems that antiquities are discovered more than expected either on public land, which is not subject to land speculation, or in a densely populated zone with many small fragmented plots. In the other areas, even if it is suspected that they exist, antiquities do not come to light as often as would be expected and it seems as though they can 'hide' more easily.

The buildable space is where the widest chronological and typological variety of finds is located. However, there is not a uniform distribution of these characteristics. Prehistoric antiquities are located exclusively in the zone with a low f.a.r. and m.p.h., whereas Classical antiquities are located in areas with a high f.a.r. and m.p.h., usually with deep foundations and building plans which are thwarted due to the presence of antiquities. Roman finds originate principally from the public spaces of the city, mainly around contemporary roads which follow ancient routes. Other periods, such as the Byzantine and post-Byzantine eras, are represented by sites mostly in the buildable zone and where there are medium and high f.a.r. and m.p.h.

The buildable zone boasts the widest typological variety of archaeological resources, principally in zones with a high f.a.r. and m.p.h. Since the ancient road network is in many cases covered by the modern one, roads and segments of the water supply network are found more often at archaeological excavations around roads in the city. Another characteristic example is finds from graves, which originate from the three cemeteries of the city.

Principally discovered in the zone with high buildings and deep foundations, they are subject to pressure for completion of construction projects, so preserving them in this environment is even more difficult than elsewhere.

The dilemma of the management of finds, mainly of architectural remains, and their preservation status after the completion of rescue excavation is not resolved in the same way throughout the city, and is determined by varying economic and social pressures. In general, the reburial of antiquities is the most usual outcome of an archaeological investigation and is among the most desirable protection methods. However, this approach is not uniformly distributed. The architectural remains which are found in public spaces have a better chance of being reburied after an investigation, a gift to the next generations of inhabitants and researchers. Conversely, the standing remains from rescue excavations on private land are removed or demolished more often than expected.

The aim of detecting potential archaeological surfaces is to identify areas on which future archaeological research is expected to focus, in this case, the buildable zone, particularly the areas with a high f.a.r. There more than anywhere else will stakeholders, planners and archaeologists have to reconsider their plans for development and cultural resource management.

These conclusions do not only help us understand the interaction of ancient deposits and the modern construction industry in the palimpsest of the city, and the contemporary urban fabric. They are also useful on an operational level in restoring the equilibrium between the various regulations of the city, both in the buildable/private and the unbuildable/public spaces, but also within the buildable space itself, where various regulations form a different picture of construction from area to area. In the light of this data the introduction of a new building regulation, that is, maximum permitted excavation depth, is proposed.

The idea of introducing a new building regulation was not predetermined from the outset of this study. It was conceived during the course of the study and as a reaction to the incapability of the existing building regulations to sufficiently manage the archaeological palimpsest of the city.

Maximum permitted excavation depth could constitute an important building regulation. Intended excavation depth is not the same everywhere in the city. However, it influences the likelihood of destroying archaeological strata in a significant way, and, in fact, as it increases, so does the likelihood of encountering the archaeological horizon of an ancient site. On the other hand, there is no corresponding reason for restricting excavation depth in the non-archaeological space. An awareness of the maximum known depth without archaeological deposits at a site can contribute to the prevention of encountering antiquities.

This approach, although it may seem rational and in their best interests, does not appear to prevail among the choices of private investors in the city. Therefore, while in public spaces both the figures concerning excavations in general and those concerning archaeological excavations in particular show that intended excavation depth and maximum known depth without archaeological deposits virtually coincide, thus giving the builder the opportunity to avoid antiquities completely, in the buildable zone the opposite happens. Not only do private individuals not take into account the possibility of finding antiquities during the course of the excavation of their building plots, but also, ironically, archaeological excavations have a greater intended excavation depth than non-archaeological excavations. In other words, a large part of the excavation coincides with the archaeological layer, even though this could be avoided. Obviously, if owners of such plots wished to avoid entirely the intervention of the Archaeological Service and whatever costs in time and money might be incurred, they would have to make significant changes to their initial plans and take into consideration the possibility of antiquities being found on their property. Since this does not happen, private individuals suffer delays, changes to their initial plans, increases in their budgets and hardship. Another fate, though, awaits the antiquities which come to light. The rescue excavation and what follows is the last resort, since the antiquities are safer when they remain unknown and buried in the soil, as they have done for thousands of years.

As a consequence, maximum permitted excavation depth is regarded as a meaningful building regulation. Once it is implemented, along with the use of updated predictive models, it will have a catalytic effect on the chances of encountering the archaeological horizon of an ancient site and disturbing archaeological layers.

6.2 GIS in the city: Practical Applications & Future Research

The results of this application can be used in a variety of ways, both on an operational level, when conducting archaeological research and monitoring construction activity in the city, and, on a theoretical level, in a general discussion regarding the role of city planning in cultural heritage management.

Among the practical matters is the recording of data from excavational works (existence of antiquities or not, foundation depth, depth of discovery of antiquities, delay due to investigation, length of rescue excavation, works in buildable or unbuildable space, building regulations, etc.). The problematic maintenance of records by public services is a restriction on this kind of research. On the other hand, when full use is made of the mass of information, the archaeological physiognomy of a contemporary city and its implications for the functions of the city can be clarified. Weaknesses in the way research and planning are conducted are identified and ways of re-examining and eradicating them can be proposed. The restoration

of a balance between the various parameters of the city is sought both in the private as well as the public zones, but also within the private zone, where varying regulations form a different picture from area to area.

The adaptation of the building regulations to the likelihood of finding antiquities in particular areas and at particular depths, and incorporating the maximum permitted excavation depth into them, contributes positively to construction plans and works. In addition, it can lead to further study and research in order to identify other ways of reconciling citizens with the historical background of their city, without restricting their plans or the development of the city.

In this way, the tension which usually characterises the relationships between archaeologists, city planners, contractors, landowners, private individuals and institutional bodies is minimalised. All those involved can have access to a bank of basic archaeological and city planning information, which will inform them during the initial phase of decision making and protect them from taking decisions that they might later be forced to reverse. They can all continue to play their roles within the institutional environment, which adapts as necessary without giving in to pressure. A condition for this ambition to be realised is the updating of the database and the exchange of information between the stakeholders involved, so that the picture of the city portrayed by the City Plan always reflects reality in a reliable and comprehensive way.

To this end, the contribution of modern technology, particularly that of GIS, proves to be invaluable. By making use of more specialised archaeological parameters in combination with city planning data, it is possible to construct even more advanced models. Experts from all the fields involved admit that computer applications need to be adopted, and some have already done so or collaborate with others who use such technology.

Among the benefits is a more complete implementation of the law, regarding both the preservation of antiquities and planning and sustainable development. Moreover, flexibility in the manipulation of data using new technologies will contribute to a smooth transition to the implementation of the new way of issuing planning permission (Law 4030/2011), which has been in force since March 1st 2012, and is characterised by a reduction in the time required, a simplification of the procedure and the completion of transactions electronically.

Besides, the proposed methodology can be employed for this purpose in other contemporary cities built over ancient ones, whether in Greece or elsewhere, since it is based on procedures which are simple and fast and can be immediately implemented within the framework of existing administrative structures and legal constraints. Naturally, a necessary condition for this technology to be adopted in a city or a country is that private individuals and the institutional bodies of the country are inspired by a desire to preserve cultural heritage and implement their corresponding national legislation.

On a theoretical level, the inhabitants of a city are placed at the centre of a complete plan for the space in which they live and work. Their personal and family development and prosperity are not inhibited, and their building plans are restricted in a way that does not harm them without them expecting it. Informed citizens do not benefit only because they are informed about the possibility of finding archaeological resources on their property and at a particular depth. They also recognise the historical background of their land, are reconciled with their cultural environment and increase the subjective value that they attach to their town. Their interest in history and art is renewed and their need for respect for and the maintenance of their cultural identity is satisfied. The historical complexity of the city is highlighted and the role of planning is redefined from the simple technical process of producing plans to an integrated procedure for intervening in the decision making process.

The awkwardness which is associated with discovering antiquities during construction projects may be interpreted as being due to the fact that the implications (and 'invisible relationships') of the coexistence of the archaeological palimpsest of a city and its contemporary needs and functions have yet to be studied. This mostly concerns those sections of the palimpsest which have not yet come to light, and whose existence was suspected or unknown. This study demonstrates that the unknown but potential layers of the palimpsest can be predicted, and the contribution of existing archaeological research to the planning and developmental prospects of a city is decisive, even if this often happens without it being noticed. Indeed, the adaptation and enhancement of building regulations based on archaeological findings, as is proposed, does not contribute only to effective cultural heritage management, but also to the development of innovative and creative planning solutions on the part of city planners and the realisation on the part of the inhabitants that their city and themselves with it have an identity and defined rules.

However, in the process of answering the research questions of this study, new questions have been raised and, naturally, with its completion not only does it not reach a definitive end, but also paves the way for future research. Advanced technologies, such as Fuzzy Logic (Kosko, 1994; Gillings, 1998; Hatzinikolaou, 2006; Runz et al 2007; Hatzinikolaou et al, 2003) and Network Analysis (Brughmans et al 2012) are methodological approaches which are implemented through a GIS environment and exploit the ever-growing range of applications within it and the parallel increase in users' demands.

Nevertheless, the extensive and intensive use of new technologies in no way constitutes a panacea for the resolution of all the questions and all the problems of a city and its inhabitants. Even experienced users of information systems will never succeed in understanding the information they are processing if they remain in their offices. Strolling around the city, soaking up stimuli with all the senses and communicating with others, apart from the psychological lift and physical relaxation these activities offer, constitute inexhaustible sources of information and ways of generating fresh thoughts and questions.

References

Aldenderfer, M. 1998: Quantitative methods in archaeology: a review of recent trends and developments. *Journal of Archaeological Research 6/2*, 91-120.

Al-Kodmany, K. 1999: Using visualization techniques for enhancing public participation in planning and design: process, implementation, and evaluation. *Landscape and Urban Planning 45*, 37-45.

Allen, K.M.S., S.W. Green & E.B.W. Zubrow (eds) 1990: *Interpreting Space: GIS and archaeology*. London: Taylor & Francis.

Allen, Sydoriak K. 2000: Considerations of scale in modeling settlement patterns using GIS: An Iroquois example. Westcott, K. L. & R. J. Brandon (eds): *Practical Applications of GIS for Archaeologists: A Predictive Modeling Toolkit*. London: Taylor & Francis, 101-112.

Amores, F., L. Garcia, V. Hurtado & M. C. Rodriguez–Bobada, 1999: Geographic Information Systems and Archaeological Resource Management in Andalusia (Spain). Barceló, J. A., I. Briz & A. Vila (eds): *New techniques for old times – CAA 98 – Computer Applications and Quantitative Methods in Archaeology: Proceedings of the 26th conference, Barcelona, March 1998*. Oxford, BAR Publishing, 351-356.

Amores, F., L. Garcia, V. Hurtado, H. Márquez & C. Rodriguez-Bobada, 2000: An exploratory GIS approach to Andalusian Archaeological Heritage Records. Lockyear K., T. J. T. Sly & V. M. Mihailesku–Birliba (eds): *CAA 96: computer applications and quantitative methods in archaeology*. Oxford: BAR Publishing, 101-116.

Anschuetz, K.F., R.H. Wilhusen & C.L. Scheick, 2001: An archaeology of landscapes: Perspectives and Directions. *Journal of Archaeological Research 9/2*, 157-211.

Anselin, L. 1993a: Exploratory Spatial Data Analysis and Geographic Information Systems. *Paper prepared for presentation at the DOSES/Eurostat Workshop on New Tools for Spatial Analysis, Lisbon, November 18-20 1993*. http://rri.wvu.edu/pdffiles/wp9329.pdf (31-5-2011).

Anselin, L. 1993b: The Moran Scatterplot as an ESDA tool to assess local instability in spatial association. *Paper prepared for presentation at the GISDATA Specialist Meeting on GIS and Spatial Analysis, The Netherlands, December 1-5 1993*. http://rri.wvu.edu/pdffiles/wp9330.pdf (31-5-2011).

Aravantinos, 1992: Αραβαντινός, Αθ. 1992: Δυναμικές αλληλεξαρτήσεις στον αστικό χώρο. Συμβολή στην κατανόηση και το σχεδιασμό οργάνωσης των πολεοδομικών λειτουργιών. Κουτσόπουλος Κ. (επιμ.): *Ανάπτυξη και σχεδιασμός: Διεπιστημονική προσέγγιση*. Αθήνα: εκδ. Παπαζήση, 323-333.

Arroyo-Bishop, D. & M.T. Lantada Zarzosa 1995: To be or not to be: will an oject-space-time GIS/AIS become a scientific reality or end up an archaeological entity? Lock G. & Z. Stančič (eds): *Archaeology and Geographical Information Systems: a European Agenda*. London: Taylor & Francis, 43-53.

Augspurger, C.K. & S.E. Franson 1987: Wind dispersal of artificial fruits varying in mass, area, and morphology. *Ecology 68/1*, 27-42.

Avern, G.J. 2001: A new Technique for Recording Archaeological Excavations: Research Progress Report. Stančič, Z. & T. Veljanovski (eds): *Computing Archaeology for Understanding the Past CAA2000. Computer Applications and Quantitative Methods in Archaeology*. Oxford: BAR Publishing - BAR International Series 931, 3-8.

Baena Preysler, J., C. Blasco Bosqued, J. Expiago & A. Rio, 1999: Geographic information systems and archaeology: methodological aspects of the presentation and display of results. Gillings, M., D. Mattingly & J. van Dalen (eds): *Geographical Information Systems and Landscape Archaeology*. Oxford the practice of Computer: Oxbow Books, 132-137.

Bakirtzis, 2004: Μπακιρτζής, Χ. (επιμ.) 2004: *Αρχαιολογικές έρευνες και μεγάλα δημόσια έργα. Αρχαιολογική συνάντηση Εργασίας, Επταπύργιο 18-20 Σεπτεμβρίου 2003*. Αθήνα: Υπουργείο Πολιτισμού, Επιτροπή Παρακολούθησης Μεγάλων Έργων.

Barceló, J.A., O. de Castro, D. Travet & O. Vicente, 2003: A 3D model of an archaeological excavation. Doerr, M. & A. Sarris (eds): *CAA 2002: The digital heritage of archaeology*. Athens: Archive of Monuments and Publications, 85-89.

Beex, W. 2004: Use and abuse of digital terrain/elevation models. Ausserer, K.F., W. Börner, M. Goriany & L. Karlhuber-Vöckl (eds): *Enter the Past. The E-way into the four Dimensions of Cultural Heritage. CAA 2003, Computer Applications and Quantitative Methods in Archaeology*. Oxford: BAR Publishing - BAR International Series 1227, 240-242.

Bevan, A. & J. Conolly, 2009: Modelling spatial heterogeneity and nonstationarity in artifact-rich landscapes. *Journal of Archaeological Science 36*, 956-964.

Bigliardi, G. 2007: Il sistema informativo territoriale archeologico della città di Parma. *Archeologia e Calcolatori 18,* 75-100.

Binford, S. R. & L. R. Binford (eds) 1968: *New perspectives in archeology.* Chicago, Aldine.

Bintliff, J. 1991: The contribution of an Annaliste/structural history approach to archaeology. Bintliff, J. (ed.): *The Annales School and Archaeology.* Leicester: Leicester University Press, 1-33.

Bintliff, J. L., P. Howard, A. M.Snodgrass & O. T. P. K. Dickinson, 2007: *Testing the hinterland: The work of the Boeotia Survey (1989-1991) in the southern approaches to the city of Thespiai.* McDonald Institute for Archeological Research.

Bis Worch, C. 2007: Preventive archaeology in Luxemburg. Legislation and reality. Bozoki Ernyey, K. (ed.): *European Preventive Archaeology: Papers of the EPAC Meeting, Vilnius 2004.* Hungary – Council of Europe -National Office of Cultural Heritage, 155-160.

Biswell, S., L. Cropper, J. Evans, V. Gaffney & P. Leach, 1995: GIS and excavation: a cautionary tale from Shepton Mallet, Somerset, England. Lock, G. & Z. Stančič (eds): *Archaeology and Geographical Information Systems: a European Agenda.* London: Taylor & Francis, 269-285.

Blalock, H. M. Jr, 1979: *Social statistics.* Auckland: Mc Graw Hill Book Company.

Blasco Bosqued, C., J. Baena Preysler & J. Expiago, 1996: The role of GIS in the management of archaeological data: an example of application for the Spanish administration. Aldenderfer, M. & H.D.G. Maschner (eds): *Anthropology, Space, and Geographic Information Systems.* New York- Oxford: Oxford University Press, 190- 201.

Börner, W. 2001: Vienna Archaeological GIS (VAGIS): A Short Outline of a New System for the Stadtarchäologie Wien. Stančič, Z. & T. Veljanovski (eds): *Computing Archaeology for Understanding the Past CAA2000. Computer Applications and Quantitative Methods in Archaeology.* Oxford: BAR Publishing - BAR International Series 931, 149-152.

Börner, W. 2002: 2000 years of town planning in Vienna. Burenhult, G. (ed.): *Archaeological Informatics: Pushing the Envelope CAA2001. Computer Applications and Quantitative Methods in Archaeology.* Oxford: BAR Publishing - BAR International Series 1016, 13-19.

Bozoki Ernyey, K. (ed.) 2007a: *European Preventive Archaeology: Papers of the EPAC Meeting, Vilnius 2004.* Hungary – Council of Europe -National Office of Cultural Heritage.

Bozoki Ernyey, K. 2007b: Preface. Bozoki Ernyey, K. (ed.): *European Preventive Archaeology: Papers of the EPAC Meeting, Vilnius 2004.* Hungary – Council of Europe -National Office of Cultural Heritage, 11-12.

Brainerd, G.W. 1951: The place of chronological ordering in archaeological analysis. *American Antiquity XVI/4,* 301-313.

Brown, P.E. & B.H. Rubin, 1982: Patterns of desert resource use: an integrated approach to settlement analysis. Brown, P.E. & C.L. Stone (eds): *Granite Reef: a study in desert archaeology.* Tempe: Arizona State University, 267-305.

Brughmans, T., L. Isaksen & G. Earl 2012: Connecting the Dots: an Introduction to Critical Approaches in Archaeological Network Analysis. Zhou, M., I. Romanowska, Z. Wu, P. Xu & P. Verhagen (eds.): *Revive the Past. Computer Applications and Quantitative Methods in Archaeology (CAA). Proceedings of the 39th International Conference, Beijing, April 12-16 2011.* Amsterdam: Pallas Publications, 359-369.

Bureš, M. 2007: From planning application to the final report in the Czech Republic. Bozoki Ernyey, K. (ed.): *European Preventive Archaeology: Papers of the EPAC Meeting, Vilnius 2004.* Hungary – Council of Europe -National Office of Cultural Heritage, 19-32.

Burrough P.A. & R. A. McDonnell, 1998: *Principles of geographical information systems.* Oxford: Oxford University Press.

Burrough P.A. 1993: *Principles of geographical information systems for land resources assessment.* Oxford: Clarendon Press.

Cattani, M., A. Fiorini & B. Rondelli, 2004: Computer applications for a reconstruction of archaeological stratigraphy as a predictive model in urban and territorial contexts. Ausserer, K.F., W. Börner, M. Goriany & L. Karlhuber-Vöckl (eds): *Enter the Past. The E-way into the four Dimensions of Cultural Heritage. CAA 2003, Computer Applications and Quantitative Methods in Archaeology.* Oxford: BAR Publishing - BAR International Series 1227, 299-303.

Chadwick, A.J. 1978: A computer simulation of Mycenaean settlement. Hodder I. (ed.): *Simulation studies in archaeology.* Cambridge: Cambridge University Press, 47-57.

Chadwick, A.J. 1979: Settlement simulation. Renfrew, C. & D. Cooke (eds): *Transformations: Mathematical approaches to culture change.* New York: Academic Press, 237-255.

Charatzopoulou, 2001: Χαρατζοπούλου, Κ. 2001: Οι εφαρμογές πληροφορικής στο Αρχαιολογικό Ίδρυμα Ρόδου: συντονισμένες υπηρεσίες για την υποστήριξη του σύνθετου έργου μιας αρχαιολογικής υπηρεσίας: Συνέντευξη με τον κ. Νίκο Ζαρίφη. *Αρχαιολογία & Τέχνες, 79,* 124-126.

Chartrand, J., J. Richards & B. Vyner, 1993: Bridging the urban-rural gap. GIS and the York Environs Project. Andresen, J., T. Madsen & I. Scollar (eds): *Computing the past: computer applications and quantitative methods in archaeology CAA92*. Århus: Århus University Press, 159-166.

Chatzimbiros, 1997: Χατζημπίρος, Κ. 1997: Περιβαλλοντική διάσταση της αστικής ανάπτυξης. Αραβαντινός, Αθ. Ι. (επιμ.): *Πολεοδομικός σχεδιασμός για μια βιώσιμη ανάπτυξη του αστικού χώρου*. Συμμετρία, Αθήνα, 477-4.

Chiang, C.-H. & Y.-C. Liu, 2012:. Mapping Prehistoric Building Structures by Visualising Archaeological Data and Applying Spatial Statistics: a Case Study from Taiwan. Zhou, M., I. Romanowska, Z. Wu, P. Xu & P. Verhagen (eds.): *Revive the Past. Computer Applications and Quantitative Methods in Archaeology (CAA). Proceedings of the 39th International Conference, Beijing, April 12-16 2011*. Amsterdam: Pallas Publications, 296-306.

Chorianopoulos, 2006: Χωριανόπουλος, Ι. 2006: Η ποιοτική έρευνα με ημιδομημένες συνεντεύξεις και το πρόβλημα της εισόδου στο πεδίο: Η περίπτωση της αστικής πολιτικής στην Ευρωπαϊκή Ένωση. Ιωσηφίδης, Θ. & Μ. Σπυριδάκης (επιμ.): *Ποιοτική κοινωνική έρευνα: μεθοδολογικές προσεγγίσεις και ανάλυση δεδομένων*. Αθήνα: Κριτική, 157-175.

Christophilopoulos, 1988: Χριστοφιλόπουλος, Δ. 1988: *Γενικός Οικοδομικός Κανονισμός (Ν. 1577/85 όπως τροποποιήθηκε με το Ν. 1772/88)*. Αθήνα: Αφοί Π. Σάκκουλα.

Christophilopoulos, 1997: Χριστοφιλόπουλος, Δ. 1997: Το νομοθετικό και οργανωτικό πλαίσιο του πολεοδομικού σχεδιασμού στην Ελλάδα. Αραβαντινός, Α.Ι. (επιμ.): *Πολεοδομικός σχεδιασμός για μια βιώσιμη ανάπτυξη του αστικού χώρου*. Αθήνα: Συμμετρία, 95-115.

Christophilopoulos, 2002: Χριστοφιλόπουλος, Δ. 2002: *Πολιτιστικό Περιβάλλον – Χωρικός Σχεδιασμός και Βιώσιμη Ανάπτυξη*. Αθήνα: Π.Ν.Σάκκουλας.

Church, T., R.J. Brandon & G.R. Burgett, 2000: GIS applications in archaeology: Method in search of theory. Westcott, K. L. & R. J. Brandon (eds): *Practical Applications of GIS for Archaeologists: A Predictive Modeling Toolkit*. London: Taylor & Francis, 135-155.

Clarke, D. 1973: Archaeology: the loss of innocence. *Antiquity XLVII*, 6-18.

Claßen, E. & A. Zimmermann, 2004: Tesselations and triangulations- Understanding early Neolithic social networks. Ausscrer, K.F., W. Börner, M. Goriany & L. Karlhuber-Vöckl (eds): *Enter the Past. The E-way into the four Dimensions of Cultural Heritage. CAA 2003, Computer Applications and Quantitative Methods in Archaeology*. Oxford: BAR Publishing - BAR International Series 1227, 467-471.

Cliff, A.D. & J.K. Ord, 1981: *Spatial processes*. London: Pion.

Collective Volume, 2001: *Η ανάδειξη του περιβάλλοντος ως παράγοντα ανάπτυξης στο μεσογειακό χώρο: Τελική σύνθεση εργασιών*. Αθήνα.

Connoly, J. & M. Lake, 2006: *Geographical Information Systems in Archaeology*. Cambridge University Press, Cambridge.

Constantinidis, D. 2001: Introspective sitescaping with GIS. Stančič, Z. & T. Veljanovski (eds): *Computing Archaeology for Understanding the Past CAA2000. Computer Applications and Quantitative Methods in Archaeology*. Oxford: BAR Publishing - BAR International Series 931, 165-172.

Constantinidis, D. 2007: Time to look for a Temporal GIS. Figueiredo, A. & G. Leite Velho (eds): *The world is in your eyes - Proceedings of the XXXIII Computer Applications in Archaeology Conference: Tomar March 2005*. Tomar: CAAPortugal, 407-411.

Contreras, D. A. 2009: Reconstructing landscape at Chavin de Huantar, Peru: A GIS- based approach. *Journal of Archaeological Science 36*, 1006-1017.

Council of Europe, 1992: *European Convention on the Protection of the Archaeological Heritage (Revised), European Treaty No 143*, http://conventions.coe.int/treaty/en/treaties/html/143.htm

Cressie, N.A.C. 1993: *Statistics for spatial data*. New York: John Wiley & Sons.

Csáki, G., E. Jerem & F. Redö, 1995: Data recording and GIS applications in landscape and intra-site analysis: case studies in progress at the Archaeological Institute of the Hungarian Academy of Sciences. Lock, G. & Z. Stančič (eds): *Archaeology and Geographical Information Systems: a European Agenda*. London: Taylor & Francis, 85-99.

D'Andrea, A., R. De Nicola & A. Giordano, 1999: The Eurialo project: a vector GIS for the integrated management of the archaeological data of Pontecagnano (Italy). Barceló, J. A., I. Briz & A. Vila (eds): *New techniques for old times – CAA 98 – Computer Applications and Quantitative Methods in Archaeology: Proceedings of the 26th conference, Barcelona, March 1998*. Oxford, BAR Publishing, 145-152.

Dalla Bona, L. 2000: Protecting cultural resources through forest management planning in Ontario using archaeological predictive modeling. Westcott, K. L. & R. J. Brandon (eds): *Practical Applications of GIS for Archaeologists: A Predictive Modeling Toolkit*. London: Taylor & Francis, 73-99.

de Blij, H. J. 1995: *The Earth: An introduction to its physical and human geography*. N. York: J. Wiley and Sons Inc.

Dejeant-Pons, M. 2006: The European Landscape Convention. *Landscape Research 31/4*, 363-384.

Derruau, M. 1987: *Ανθρωπογεωγραφία*, μετ. Γ. Πρεβελάκη. Αθήνα: ΜΙΕΤ.

Dertilis, 1996: Δερτιλής, Γ.Β. 1996: *Αεί παίδες απαίδευτοι: Είκοσι τρία σχόλια περί εθνικισμού, πλούτου και παιδείας.* Αθήνα: Καστανιώτη.

Diamanti, N. G., G. N. Tsokas, P. I. Tsourlos & A. Vafidis, 2005: Intergrated interpretation of geophysical data in the archaeological site of Europos (northern Greece). *Archaeological Prospection 12,* 79-91.

Diappi, L. (ed.) 2004: *Evolving cities: geocomputation in territorial planning.* Aldershot: Ashgate.

Diaz-Andreu, M. & T. C. Champion, 1996: Nationalism and archaeology in Europe: an introduction. Diaz-Andreu, M. & T.C. Champion (eds): *Nationalism and Archaeology in Europe.* London: University College London Press, 1- 23.

Djurič, B. 2007: Preventive archaeology and archaeological service in Slovenia. Bozoki Ernyey, K. (ed.): *European Preventive Archaeology: Papers of the EPAC Meeting, Vilnius 2004.* Hungary – Council of Europe -National Office of Cultural Heritage, 180-186.

Doerr, M. & D. Iorizzo, 2008: The Dream of a Global Knowledge Network—A New Approach. *Journal on Computing and Cultural Heritage 1/1,* 5:1-5:23.

Dolff Bonekämper, G. 2009: The social and spatial frameworks of heritage – What is new in the Faro Convention? Council Of Europe Publishing (ed.): *Heritage and beyond.* Strasbourg: Council of Europe publishing, 69-74.

Doneus, M. & W. Neubauer, 2004: Digital recording of stratigraphic excavations. Ausserer, K.F., W. Börner, M. Goriany & L. Karlhuber-Vöckl, (eds): *Enter the Past. The E-way into the four Dimensions of Cultural Heritage. CAA 2003, Computer Applications and Quantitative Methods in Archaeology.* Oxford: BAR Publishing - BAR International Series 1227, 113-116.

Doran, J.E. & F.R. Hodson 1975: *Mathematics and computers in archaeology.* Harvard: Harvard University Press.

Dore, C. D. & L.A.Wandsnider, 2006: Modeling for management in a compliance world. Mehrer, W. & K. L. Westcott (eds): *GIS and Archaeological Site Location Modeling.* Boca Raton: Taylor & Francis, 75-96.

Dosse, Fr. 1993: *Η ιστορία σε ψίχουλα: Από τα Annales στη "Νέα Ιστορία".* μετ. Αγγ. Βλαχοπούλου. Ηράκλειο: Παν. Εκδ. Κρήτης.

Drennan, R.D. 1996: *Statistics for Archaeologists.* New York: Plenum Press.

Ebert, D. 2002: The potential of Geostatistics in the analysis of fieldwalking data. Wheatley, D., G. Earl & S. Poppy (eds): *Contemporary themes in archaeological computing.* Oxford: Oxbow Books, 84- 89.

Ebert, J.I. 2000: The state of the art in "inductive" predictive modeling: seven big mistakes (and lots of smaller ones). Westcott, K. L. & R. J. Brandon (eds):

Practical Applications of GIS for Archaeologists: A Predictive Modeling Toolkit. London: Taylor & Francis, 129-134.

Evans, B. 1997: From town planning to environmental planning. Blowers, A. & B. Evans (eds): *Town Planning into the 21st century.* London and N. York: Routledge, 1-14.

Fairclough, G. 2003: "The long chain": Archaeology, Historical Landscape Characterization and the time depth in the landscape. Palang, H. & G. Fry (eds): *Landscape interfaces: cultural heritage in changing landscapes.* Dordrecht/ Boston/ London: Kluwer Academic Publishers, 295-318.

Farinetti, E. & L. Sigalos, 2002: Detailed topography and surface survey. What is the point? Tanagra city survey 2000. Burenhult, G. (ed.): *Archaeological Informatics: Pushing the Envelope CAA2001. Computer Applications and Quantitative Methods in Archaeology.* Oxford: BAR Publishing - BAR International Series 1016, 385-391.

Farinetti, E. 2011: *Boeotian landscapes: a GIS-based study for the reconstruction and interpretation of the archaeological datasets of ancient Boeotia.* Oxford: BAR Publishing.

Fernández, J.I.F. & J.M.M. Solé, 2007: FormaTarraconis? GIS use for urban archaeology. Figueiredo, A. & G. Leite Velho (eds): *The world is in your eyes - Proceedings of the XXXIII Computer Applications in Archaeology Conference: Tomar March 2005.* Tomar: CAAPortugal, 423-427.

Fisher, M. D. 1994: *Applications in Computing for Social Anthropologists.* London & N. York: Routledge.

Fisher, P., C. Farrelly & A. Maddocks, 1997: Spatial analysis of visible areas from the Bronge age cairns of Mull. *Journal of Archaeological Science 24,* 581-592.

Fleming, A. 2006: Post-processual Landscape Archaeology: a Critique. *Cambridge Archaeological Journal 16/3,* 267-280.

Fletcher, R. 2008: Some spatial analyses of chalcolithic settlement in southern Israel. *Journal of Archaeological Science, 35,* 2048-2058.

Fronza, V., A. Nardini & M. Valenti, 2003: An integrated information system for archaeological data management: latest developments. Doerr, M. & A. Sarris (eds): *CAA 2002: The digital heritage of archaeology.* Athens: Archive of Monuments and Publications, 147-153.

Fronza, V., A. Nardini, F. Salzotti & M. Valenti, 2001: A GIS Solution for Excavations: Experience of the Siena University LIAAM. Stančič, Z. & T. Veljanovski (eds): *Computing Archaeology for Understanding the Past CAA2000. Computer Applications and Quantitative Methods in Archaeology.* Oxford: BAR Publishing - BAR International Series 931, 173-178.

Gaffney, V. & P.M. van Leusen, 1995: Postscript: GIS, environmental determinism and archaeology. Lock,

G. & Z. Stančič (eds): *Archaeology and Geographical Information Systems: a European Agenda*. London: Taylor & Francis, 367-382.

Gaffney, V. & Z. Stančič 1991: *GIS approaches to regional analysis: a case study of the island of Hvar*. Ljubljana: Filozofska Fakulteta.

Georgopoulou Verra, 1997: Γεωργοπούλου – Βέρρα, Μ. 1997: Η Χριστιανική Πάτρα και τα μνημεία της. *Η πολιτιστική φυσιογνωμία της Πάτρας*. Πάτρα: Εκδόσεις Πανεπιστημίου Πατρών, 35-55.

Gialis et al 2006: Γκιάλης, Σ., Α. Γονιδάκης, Π. Κανελλέας & Π. Κοντοζούδης, 2006: Ανάπτυξη εφαρμογών Γ.Σ.Π. για Οργανισμούς Τοπικής Αυτοδιοίκησης: η περίπτωση του Δήμου Ρόδου. *Ηλεκτρονική Διακυβέρνηση: ο ρόλος των Γ.Σ.Π, Δ΄ Συνέδριο HellasGI, Αθήνα 4-5/5/2006. www.gipsynoise.gr/HellasGI/4oSynedrio/papers/Gialis_et_al.pdf* (20-5-2011).

Gillings, M. & K. Sbonias, 1999: Regional survey and GIS: The Boeotia project. Gillings, M., D. Mattingly & J. van Dalen (eds): *Geographical Information Systems and Landscape Archaeology*. Oxford: Oxbow Books, 35-54.

Gillings, M. 1998: Embracing uncertainty and challenging dualism in the GIS-based study of paleo-flood plain. *European Journal of Archaeology 1/1*, 117-144.

Gleeson, P. 2007: Rescue excavation in Ireland – Roads and codes. Bozoki Ernyey, K. (ed.): *European Preventive Archaeology: Papers of the EPAC Meeting, Vilnius 2004*. Hungary – Council of Europe -National Office of Cultural Heritage, 136-145.

Graves, D. 2011: The use of predictive modeling to target Neolithic settlement and occupation activity in mainland Scotland. *Journal of Archaeological Science 38*, 633-656.

Guermandi, M.P. 1999: Protection of the archaeological patrimony and G.I.S. The elaboration of an archaeological cartography aimed at the problems of territorial planning in the Emilia Romagna Region. Barceló, J. A., I. Briz & A. Vila (eds): *New techniques for old times – CAA 98 – Computer Applications and Quantitative Methods in Archaeology: Proceedings of the 26th conference, Barcelona, March 1998*. Oxford: BAR Publishing, 359-363.

Haining, R. 2003: *Spatial data analysis: theory and practice*. Cambridge: Cambridge University Press.

Halls, P.J., M. Bulling, P.C.L. White, L. Garland & S. Harris, 2001: Dirichlet neighbours: revisiting Dirichlet Tesselation for Neighbourhood Analysis. *Computers, Environment and Urban Systems 25/1*, 105-117.

Harris, T. & G. Lock, 1995: Toward an evaluation of GIS in European archaeology: the past, present and future of theory and applications. Lock, G. & Z. Stančič (eds): *Archaeology and Geographical Information Systems: a European Agenda*. London: Taylor & Francis, 349-365.

Harris, T. & G. Lock, 1996: Multi-dimensional GIS: exploratory approaches to spatial and temporal relationships within archaeological stratigraphy. Kamermans, H. & K. Fennema (eds): *Interfacing the past: Computer Applications and Quantitative Methods in Archaeology 1995*. Leiden: Institute of Prehistory, 307-316.

Harris, T.M. & G.R. Lock, 1990: The diffusion of a new technology: a perspective on the adoption of geographic information systems within UK archaeology. Allen, K.M.S., S.W. Green & E.B.W. Zubrow (eds): *Interpreting Space: GIS and archaeology*. London: Taylor & Francis, 33-53.

Hasenstab, R.J. 1996: Settlement as adaptation: Variability in Iroquois village site selection as inferred through GIS. Maschner, H.D.G. (ed.) *New Methods Old Problems; Geographic Information Systems in Modern Archaeological Research*. Carbondale, Southern Illinois University Center for Archaeological Investigations, 223-241.

Hatzinikolaou, E., T. Hatzichristos, A. Siolas & E. Mantzourani, 2003: Predicting archaeological site locations using G.I.S. and Fuzzy Logic. Doerr M. & A. Sarris (eds): *CAA 2002: The digital heritage of archaeology*. Athens: Archive of Monuments and Publications, 169-177.

Hatzinikolaou, E.G. 2006: Quantitative methods in archaeological prediction: from binary to fuzzy logic. Mehrer, W. & K. L. Westcott (eds): *GIS and Archaeological Site Location Modeling*. Boca Raton: Taylor & Francis, 437-446.

Hearnshaw, H. 1994: Psychology and displays in GIS. Hearnshaw, H.M. & D.J. Unwin (eds): *Visualization in geographic information systems*. Chichester-New York: John Wiley & Sons, 193-199.

Hermon, S. & V. Vassallo, 2012: Preventive Archaeology: Towards a Technological Integrated Solution. Zhou, M., I. Romanowska, Z. Wu, P. Xu & P. Verhagen (eds.): *Revive the Past. Computer Applications and Quantitative Methods in Archaeology (CAA). Proceedings of the 39th International Conference, Beijing, April 12-16* 2011. Amsterdam: Pallas Publications, 177-185.

Herzfeld, M. 2003: A place in history: social and monumental time in a Cretan town. Histories in their places. Low, S.M. & D. Lawrence Zúñiga (eds): *The anthropology of space and place. Locating culture*. Oxford – Malden- Victoria: Blackwell Publishing, 363-369.

Higginbottom, G., K. Simson & R. Clay, 2002: Using viewsheds wisely: developing sound methodologies from spatial analyses of megalithic monuments in western Scotland. Burenhult, G. (ed.): *Archaeological Informatics: Pushing the Envelope CAA2001. Computer Applications and Quantitative Methods in Archaeology*. Oxford: BAR Publishing - BAR International Series 1016, 53-62.

Hjaltalin, T. 2007: Preventive archaeology in Iceland. Bozoki Ernyey, K. (ed.): *European Preventive Archaeology: Papers of the EPAC Meeting, Vilnius 2004.* Hungary – Council of Europe -National Office of Cultural Heritage, 122-135.

Hodder, I. & C. Orton, 1976: *Spatial analysis in archaeology*. Cambridge: Cambridge University Press.

Hodder, I. 1993: Changing configurations: the relationship between theory and practice. Hunter, J. & I. Ralston (eds): *Archaeological Resource Management in the UK; An Introduction.* Phoenix Mill: Alan Shutton Publishing Ltd, 11-18.

Hroch, M. 1996: Epilogue. Diaz-Andreu, M. & T.C. Champion (επιμ): *Nationalism and Archaeology in Europe*. London: University College London Press, 294-299.

Huggett, J. 2000: Looking at intra-site GIS. Lockyear, K., T. J. T. Sly & V. M. Mihailesku–Birliba (eds): *CAA 96: computer applications and quantitative methods in archaeology*. Oxford: BAR Publishing, 117-122.

Huggett, J., 2013: Applications in Archaeology: Disciplinary issues: Challenging the research and practice of computer applications in research and archaeology. Earl, G., T. Sly, A. Chrysanthi, P. Murrieta-Flores, C. Papadopoulos, I. Romanowska, & D. Wheatley (eds): *Archaeology in the Digital Era Papers from the 40th Annual Conference of Computer Applications and Quantitative Methods in Archaeology (CAA), Southampton, 26-29 March 2012.* Amsterdam, Amsterdam: University Press, 13-24.

Hunter, M. 1981: The preconditions of Preservation: a historical perspective. Lowenthal, D. & M. Binney (eds): *Our past before use: Why do we save it?* London: Temple Smith, 22-32.

Johnston K., J. M. Ver Hoef, K. Krivoruchko & N. Lucas, 2001: *Using ArcGISTM Geostatistical Analyst.* Redlands: ESRI.

Kagkarakis, 2005: Καγκαράκης, Κ. 2005: Προς μια ανάπτυξη με πυξίδα την ποιότητα. Ρόκος, Δ. (επιμ.): *Περιβάλλον και Ανάπτυξη: Διαλεκτικές σχέσεις και διεπιστημονικές προσεγγίσεις*. Αθήνα: Εναλλακτικές Εκδόσεις, 131-147.

Kakouris, 2004a: Κακούρης, Ι. 2004: Συζήτηση επί των παρεμβάσεων. Μπακιρτζής, Χ. (επιμ.): *Αρχαιολογικές έρευνες και μεγάλα δημόσια έργα. Αρχαιολογική συνάντηση Εργασίας, Επταπύργιο 18-20 Σεπτεμβρίου 2003.* Αθήνα: Υπουργείο Πολιτισμού, Επιτροπή Παρακολούθησης Μεγάλων Έργων, 450-452.

Kakouris, 2004b: Κακούρης, Ι. 2004: Διεθνής πρακτική και μεγάλα έργα. Μπακιρτζής, Χ. (επιμ.): *Αρχαιολογικές έρευνες και μεγάλα δημόσια έργα. Αρχαιολογική συνάντηση Εργασίας, Επταπύργιο 18-20 Σεπτεμβρίου 2003.* Αθήνα: Υπουργείο Πολιτισμού, Επιτροπή Παρακολούθησης Μεγάλων Έργων, 496-501.

Kamermans, H. 2006: Problems in Paleolithic land evaluation: a cautionary tale. Mehrer, W. & K. L. Westcott (eds): *GIS and Archaeological Site Location Modeling*. Boca Raton: Taylor & Francis, 97-122.

Kantner, J. 2008: The archaeology of regions: from discrete analytical toolkit to ubiquitous spatial perspective. *Journal of Archaeological Research 16*, 37-81.

Kardamitsi Adami, 1996: Καρδαμίτση Αδάμη, Μ. (επιμ.) 1996: *Σταμάτης Βούλγαρης, Ο πρώτος Έλληνας πολεοδόμος: Τα κείμενά του*. Αθήνα: Libro ΕΠΕ.

Karydis, 1991: Καρύδης, Δ. Ν. 1991: *Ανάγνωση Πολεοδομίας: η κοινωνική σημασία των χωρικών μορφών*. Αθήνα: Συμμετρία.

Katsianis, M. 2004: Stratigraphic modeling of multi-period sites using GIS: The case of Neolithic and Early Bronge Age Knossos. Ausserer, K.F., W. Börner, M. Goriany & L. Karlhuber-Vöckl (eds): *Enter the Past. The E-way into the four Dimensions of Cultural Heritage. CAA 2003, Computer Applications and Quantitative Methods in Archaeology*. Oxford: BAR Publishing - BAR International Series 1227, 304-307.

Katsianis, M., S. Tsipidis, K. Kotsakis & A. Kousoulakou, 2008: A 3D digital workflow for archaeological intra-site research using GIS. *Journal of Archaeological Science 35,* 655-667.

Kohler, T.A. & S.C. Parker 1986: Predictive models for archaeological resource location. Schiffer, M.B. (ed.): *Advances in archaeological method and theory, v.9.* New York: Academic Press, 397-452.

Kosko, B. 1994: *Fuzzy thinking: The new science of fuzzy logic*. London: Flamingo.

Koukouli Chrysanthaki, 2004: Κουκούλη Χρυσανθάκη, Χ. 2004: Προετοιμασία και διεξαγωγή των αρχαιολογικών ερευνών. Μπακιρτζής, Χ. (επιμ.): *Αρχαιολογικές έρευνες και μεγάλα δημόσια έργα. Αρχαιολογική συνάντηση Εργασίας, Επταπύργιο 18-20 Σεπτεμβρίου 2003.* Αθήνα: Υπουργείο Πολιτισμού, Επιτροπή Παρακολούθησης Μεγάλων Έργων, 477-484.

Koukouli Chrysanthaki, H., 2007: Preventive Archaeology and major public works in Greece. Bozoki Ernyey, K. (ed.): *European Preventive Archaeology: Papers of the EPAC Meeting, Vilnius 2004.* Hungary – Council of Europe -National Office of Cultural Heritage, 86-103.

Koumousi Vgenopoulou, 2006: Κουμούση Βγενοπούλου, Α. 2006: Σωστικές ανασκαφές στην Πάτρα το 1995. Συλλογικός τόμος: *Πρακτικά Α' Αρχαιολογικής Συνόδου Νότιας και Δυτικής Ελλάδας, Ιούνιος 9-12 1996.* Αθήνα: Τ.Α.Π., 117-130.

Koutsopoulos, 2000: Κουτσόπουλος, Κ. 2000: *Γεωγραφία: Μεθοδολογία και Μέθοδοι Ανάλυσης Χώρου*. Αθήνα: Συμμετρία.

Koutsopoulos, 2005: Κουτσόπουλος, Κ. 2005: Ολοκληρωμένη μεθοδολογική προσέγγιση της ανάπτυξης: Η περίπτωση των Γεωγραφικών

Συστημάτων Πληροφοριών (Γ.Σ.Π.). Ρόκος, Δ. (επιμ.): *Περιβάλλον και Ανάπτυξη: Διαλεκτικές σχέσεις και διεπιστημονικές προσεγγίσεις*. Αθήνα: Εναλλακτικές Εκδόσεις, 211-225.

Kraut, A. 2007: Preventive and rescue excavations in Estonia. The involvement of private companies. Bozoki Ernyey, K. (ed.): *European Preventive Archaeology: Papers of the EPAC Meeting, Vilnius 2004*. Hungary – Council of Europe -National Office of Cultural Heritage, 43-49.

Kritikos, 2007: Κρητικός, Γ. 2007: *Έθνος και χώρος: Προσεγγίσεις στην ιστορική γεωγραφία της σύγχρονης Ευρώπης*. Αθήνα: Μεταίχμιο.

Kvamme, K. L. 1983: *A manual for predictive site location models: examples for the Grand Junction District, Colorado. Draft submitted to the Bureau of Land Management*. Grand Junction District, Colorado.

Kvamme, K. L. 1988: Development and testing of quantitative models. Judge, W.J & L. Sebastian (eds): *Quantifying the present and predicting the past: Theory, method, and application of archaeological predictive modeling*. Denver, U.S. Department of the Interior, Bureau of Land Management Service Center, 325-428.

Kvamme, K. L. 1995: A view from across the water. Lock G. & Z. Stančič (eds): *Archaeology and Geographical Information Systems: a European Agenda*. London: Taylor & Francis, 1-14.

Kvamme, K. L. 1999: Recent directions and developments in Geographic Information Systems. *Journal of Archaeological Research 7/2*, 153-201.

Kvamme, K.L. 1989: Geographic Information Systems in regional archaeological research and data management. Schiffer M.B. (ed.): *Archaeological method and theory, v.1*. Tucson: University of Arizona Press, 139-203.

Kvamme, K.L. 1990b: One-sample tests in regional archaeological analysis: new possibilities. *American Antiquity 55/2*, 367-381.

Kvamme, K.L. 1990a: GIS algorithms and their effects on regional archaeological analysis. Allen, K.M.S., S.W. Green & E.B.W. Zubrow (eds): *Interpreting Space: GIS and archaeology*. London: Taylor & Francis, 112-125.

Kvamme, K.L. 1993: Spatial Statistics and GIS: an Integrated Approach. Andresen, J., T. Madsen & I. Scollar (eds): *Computing the past: computer applications and quantitative methods in archaeology CAA92*. Århus: Århus University Press, 91-103.

Kvamme, K.L. 1996: Investigating chipping debris scatters: GIS as an analytical engine. Maschner H.D.G. (ed.): *New Methods Old Problems; Geographic Information Systems in Modern Archaeological Research*. Carbondale: Southern Illinois University Center for Archaeological Investigations, 38-71.

Kydoniatis, 1985: Κυδωνιάτης, Σ. Π. 1985: *Αθήναι Παρελθόν και Μέλλον, τόμος Α'*. Αθήνα: Πνευματικό Κέντρο Δήμου Αθηναίων.

Lambrianides, 2002: Λαμπριανίδης, Λ. 2002: *Οικονομική Γεωγραφία: Στοιχεία θεωρίας και εμπειρικά παραδείγματα*. Αθήνα: Πατάκη.

Lambropoulou, A. & A. Moutzali, 2005: Patras town in the early Christian and Byzantine period. Sklavenitis, T.E. & K.S. Staikos (eds): *Patras: from ancient times to the present*. Athens: Kotinos Editions SA, 56-99.

Laurenza, S. & C. Putzolu, 2002: From stratigraphic unit to the mouse: a GIS based system for the excavation of historical complex. The case study of Pompeii. Burenhult, G. (ed.): *Archaeological Informatics: Pushing the Envelope CAA2001. Computer Applications and Quantitative Methods in Archaeology*. Oxford: BAR Publishing - BAR International Series 1016, 93-103.

Laurini, R. 2001: *Information systems for urban planning: a hypermedia co-operative approach*. London: Taylor & Francis.

Law 1577, 1985: Γενικός Οικοδομικός Κανονισμός. *Εφημερίς της Κυβερνήσεως της Ελληνικής Δημοκρατίας, τ. Α', 210, 18 -12-1985*.

Law 2508, 1997: Βιώσιμη οικιστική ανάπτυξη των πόλεων και οικισμών της χώρας και άλλες διατάξεις. *Εφημερίς της Κυβερνήσεως της Ελληνικής Δημοκρατίας, τ. Α', 124, 13 -6-1997*.

Law 2742, 1999: Χωροταξικός σχεδιασμός και αειφόρος ανάπτυξη και άλλες διατάξεις. *Εφημερίς της Κυβερνήσεως της Ελληνικής Δημοκρατίας, τ. Α', 207, 7-10-1999*.

Law 3028, 2002: Για την προστασία των Αρχαιοτήτων και εν γένει της Πολιτιστικής Κληρονομιάς. *Εφημερίς της Κυβερνήσεως της Ελληνικής Δημοκρατίας, τ. Α', 153, 28 -6-2002*.

Law 4030, 2011: Νέος τρόπος έκδοσης αδειών δόμησης, ελέγχου κατασκευών και λοιπές διατάξεις. *Εφημερίς της Κυβερνήσεως της Ελληνικής Δημοκρατίας, τ. Α', 249, 25-11-2011*.

Lefas, 1985: Λέφας, Π. 1985: *Αθήνα: Μία πρωτεύουσα της Ευρώπης*. Αθήνα –Γιάννενα: Εκδ. Δωδώνη.

Liroudias, 1995: Λυρούδιας, Ε. 1995: *Πολιτική και επιστήμη στον πολεοδομικό σχεδιασμό*. Αθήνα: Διόνυσος.

Lloyd, C. D. & P. M. Atkinson, 2004: Archaeology and geostatistics. *Journal of Archaeological Science 31/2*, 151-165.

Lock, G. & T. Harris, 2006: Enhancing predictive modeling: integrating location, landscape, and culture. Mehrer, W. & K. L. Westcott (eds): *GIS and Archaeological Site Location Modeling*. Boca Raton: Taylor & Francis, 41-62.

Lock, G. & Z. Stančič (eds) 1995: *Archaeology and Geographical Information Systems: a European Agenda*. London: Taylor & Francis.

Lock, G.R. & T.M. Harris, 1996: Danebury Revisited: An English Iron Age Hillfort in a Digital Landscape. Maschner, H.D.G. (ed.): *New Methods Old Problems; Geographic Information Systems in Modern Archaeological Research*. Carbondale: Southern Illinois University Center for Archaeological Investigations, 214-240.

Machácek, J. & M. Kucera, 2004: GIS and the excavation of the early medieval centre in Pohansko, Czech Republic. Ausserer, K.F., W. Börner, M. Goriany & L. Karlhuber-Vöckl, (eds): *Enter the Past. The E-way into the four Dimensions of Cultural Heritage. CAA 2003, Computer Applications and Quantitative Methods in Archaeology*. Oxford: BAR Publishing - BAR International Series 1227, 246-249.

Mackay, R. & A. Mackay, 2002: GIS-based documentation and management of Australian urban archaeology. *Strategies for the World's Cultural Heritage. Preservation in a globalised world: principles, practices and perspectives, ICOMOS 13th General Assembly and International Symposium Madrid 1-5/12/02*. www.international.icomos.org/madrid2002/actas/42.pdf (28-4-2011).

Maggi, R. 2007: The approach to preventive archaeology in Italy. Bozoki Ernyey, K. (ed.): *European Preventive Archaeology: Papers of the EPAC Meeting, Vilnius 2004*. Hungary – Council of Europe -National Office of Cultural Heritage, 146-154.

Malakasioti, 2004: Μαλακασιώτη, Z. 2004: Παρεμβάσεις σχετικά με τον προβληματισμό επί των έργων. Μπακιρτζής, Χ. (επιμ.): *Αρχαιολογικές έρευνες και μεγάλα δημόσια έργα. Αρχαιολογική συνάντηση Εργασίας, Επταπύργιο 18-20 Σεπτεμβρίου 2003*. Αθήνα: Υπουργείο Πολιτισμού, Επιτροπή Παρακολούθησης Μεγάλων Έργων, 436.

Mantzourani, E. & G. Vavouranakis, 2003: Practical and epistemological implications of recording methods: the Neolithic excavation project at Kantou-Kouphovounos, Cyprus. Doerr, M. & A. Sarris (eds): *CAA 2002: The digital heritage of archaeology*. Athens: Archive of Monuments and Publications, 355-360.

Marble, D.F. 1990: The potential methodological impact of geographic information systems on the social sciences. Allen, K.M.S., S.W. Green & E.B.W. Zubrow (eds): *Interpreting Space: GIS and archaeology*. London: Taylor & Francis, 9-21.

Marki, 2004: Μάρκη, E. 2004: Παρεμβάσεις σχετικά με τον προβληματισμό επί των έργων. Μπακιρτζής, Χ. (επιμ.): *Αρχαιολογικές έρευνες και μεγάλα δημόσια έργα. Αρχαιολογική συνάντηση Εργασίας, Επταπύργιο 18-20 Σεπτεμβρίου 2003*. Αθήνα: Υπουργείο Πολιτισμού, Επιτροπή Παρακολούθησης Μεγάλων Έργων, 437-440.

McCoy, M.D. & T.N. Ladefoged 2009: New developments in the use of spatial technology in archaeology. *Journal of Archaeological Research 17*, 263-295.

Mehrer, M.W. 2002: A GIS-based archaeological decision-support model for cultural resource management. *Archeologia e Calcolatori 13*, 125-133.

Mehrer, W. & K. L. Westcott (eds) 2006: *GIS and Archaeological Site Location Modeling*. Boca Raton: Taylor & Francis.

Mendoni, 2004: Μενδώνη, Λ. 2004: Εισηγήσεις. Μπακιρτζής, Χ. (επιμ.): *Αρχαιολογικές έρευνες και μεγάλα δημόσια έργα. Αρχαιολογική συνάντηση Εργασίας, Επταπύργιο 18-20 Σεπτεμβρίου 2003*. Αθήνα: Υπουργείο Πολιτισμού, Επιτροπή Παρακολούθησης Μεγάλων Έργων, 476.

Merlo, S. 2004: The "contemporary mind" 3D GIS as a challenge in excavation practice. Ausserer, K.F., W. Börner, M. Goriany & L. Karlhuber-Vöckl, (eds): *Enter the Past. The E-way into the four Dimensions of Cultural Heritage. CAA 2003, Computer Applications and Quantitative Methods in Archaeology*. Oxford: BAR Publishing - BAR International Series 1227, 276-280.

Meskell, L. (ed.) 1998: *Archaeology under fire. Nationalism, politics and heritage in the Eastern Mediterranean and Middle East*. London and New York: Routledge.

Miller, A.P. 1996: Digging deep: GIS in the city. Kamermans, H. & K. Fennema (eds): *Interfacing the past: Computer Applications and Quantitative Methods in Archaeology 1995*. Leiden: Institute of Prehistory, 369-376.

Miller, P. 1995: How to look good and influence people: thoughts on the design and interpretation of an archaeological GIS. Lock, G. & Z. Stančič (eds): *Archaeology and Geographical Information Systems: a European Agenda*. London: Taylor & Francis, 319-333.

Milner G. R. 1996: Interactions in prehistoric eastern North America. *Antiquity 70/270*, 992-995.

Mink, P.B., B. Jo Stokes & D. Pollack, 2006: Points vs Polygons: a test case using statewide Geographic Information System. Mehrer, W. & K. L. Westcott (eds): *GIS and Archaeological Site Location Modeling*. Boca Raton: Taylor & Francis, 219-239.

Moscati, P. 1999: GIS and archaeology: The Caere survey. Barceló, J. A., I. Briz & A. Vila (eds): *New techniques for old times – CAA 98 – Computer Applications and Quantitative Methods in Archaeology: Proceedings of the 26th conference, Barcelona, March 1998*. Oxford: BAR Publishing, 103-105.

Novakovič, P., H. Simoni & B. Music 1999: Karst dolinas: Evidence of population pressure on agricultural resources in karstic landscapes. Levau Ph. & K. Walsh (eds): *Methodological Issues in Mediterranean landscape Archaeology: Geoarchaeology*, Oxford: Oxbow, 123-134.

Nye, J. A., J. S. Link, J. A. Hare & W. J. Overholtz 2009: Changing spatial distribution of fish stocks in relation to climate and population size on the Northeast United States continental shelf. *Marine Ecology Progress Series 393*, 111-129.

Oikonomou & Petrakos, 1999: Οικονόμου, Δ. & Γ. Πετράκος, 1999: Πολιτικές οικιστικής ανάπτυξης και πολεοδομικής οργάνωσης στην Ελλάδα. Οικονόμου, Δ. & Γ. Πετράκος (επιμ.): *Η ανάπτυξη των ελληνικών πόλεων: Διεπιστημονικές προσεγγίσεις αστικής ανάλυσης και πολιτικής.* Βόλος: Πανεπιστημιακές εκδόσεις Θεσσαλίας- Gutenberg, 413-446.

Oikonomou, 1988: Οικονόμου, Δ. 1988: Σύστημα γης και κατοικίας στη μεταπολεμική Ελλάδα. Μαλούτας, Θ. & Δ. Οικονόμου (επιμ.): *Προβλήματα ανάπτυξης του κράτους πρόνοιας στην Ελλάδα.* Αθήνα: Εξάντας, 57-113.

Oikonomou, 2000: Οικονόμου, Δ. 2000: Η πολεοδομική πολιτική στη δεκαετία του '50. Δέφνερ, Α. (επιμ.): *Η Πολεοδομία στην Ελλάδα από το 1949 έως το 1974.* Βόλος: Τμήμα Μηχανικών Χωροταξίας και Περιφερειακής Ανάπτυξης – Πανεπιστήμιο Θεσσαλίας, 39- 48.

Oikonomou, 2010: Οικονόμου, Λ. 2010: «Οικόπεδα με δόσεις»: Η παραγωγή του χώρου στην αθηναϊκή περιφέρεια (1950-1960). Γιαννακόπουλος, Κ. & Γ. Γιαννιτσιώτης (επιμ.): *Αμφισβητούμενοι χώροι στην πόλη: Χωρικές προσεγγίσεις του πολιτισμού.* Αθήνα: Αλεξάνδρεια, 77-116.

Orbasli, A. 2000: *Tourists in historic towns: urban conservation and heritage management.* London: E&FN SPON.

Paliou, E., U. Lieberwirth & S. Polla (eds) 2014: *Spatial analyses and social spaces: Interdisciplinary approaches to the interpretation of prehistoric and historic built environments.* Berlin: Topoi- Berlin Studies of the Ancient World 18.

Palumbo, G. 1993: JADIS (Jordan Antiquities Database and Information System): An example of national archaeological inventory and GIS applications. Andresen, J., T. Madsen & I. Scollar (eds): *Computing the past: computer applications and quantitative methods in archaeology CAA92.* Århus: Århus University Press, 183-188.

Pantazis et al 2006: Πανταζής, Α., Π. Κυριακοπούλου & Συνεργάτες Ο.Ε. & Ε. Βακαλοπούλου, 2006: Τεύχος Ι: Ανάλυση – Διάγνωση. *Αναθεώρηση και επέκταση του Γενικού Πολεοδομικού Σχεδίου (ΓΠΣ) Δήμου Πατρέων, Φάση- Στάδιο Α: Ανάλυση- Διάγνωση- Προοπτικές- Προκαταρκτική πρόταση.* Αθήνα: Περιφερειακή Διοίκηση Αχαΐας Δήμος Πατρέων.

Papadatou Giannopoulou, 1991: Παπαδάτου Γιαννοπούλου, Χ. 1991: *Εξέλιξη του σχεδίου πόλεως των Πατρών (1829-1989).* Πάτρα: Αχαϊκές Εκδόσεις.

Papadimas & Koilias, 1998: Παπαδήμας, Ο. & Χ. Κοίλιας, 1998: *Εφαρμοσμένη Στατιστική.* Αθήνα: Εκδόσεις Νέων Τεχνολογιών.

Papadopoulos, N., A. Sarris, M. Yi & J. Kim, 2009: Urban archaeological investigations using surface 3D Ground Penetrating Radar and Electrical Resistivity Tomography methods: *Exploration Geophysics 40,* 56–68.

Papadopoulos, N.G., A. Sarris, M.C. Salvia, S. Dederix, P. Soupios & U. Dikmene, 2012: Rediscovering the small theatre and amphitheatre of ancient Ierapytna (SE Crete) by integrated geophysical methods. *Journal of Archaeological Science 39/7,* 1960-1973.

Papadopoulos, N.G., P. Tsourlos, G.N. Tsokas & A. Sarris, 2006: Two-dimensional and three-dimensional resistivity imaging in archaeological site investigation. *Archaeological Prospection 13,* 163-181.

Papageorgiou – Venetas, A. 1994: *Athens: the ancient heritage and the historic cityscape in a modern metropolis.* Athens: The Archaeological Society at Athens.

Papakonstantinou, 2003: Παπακωνσταντίνου, Β.Σ., 2003: *Εγχειρίδιο Αρχαιοκαπηλίας Επίσημης και ανεπίσημης,* Αθήνα: Περίπλους.

Papazoglou Manioudaki, 1993: Παπάζογλου Μανιουδάκη Λ. 1993: Εισηγμένη κεραμεική στους μυκηναϊκούς τάφους της Πάτρας. Zerner, C., P. Zerner & J. Winder (eds): *Proceedings of the International Conference "Wace and Blegen: pottery as evidence for trade in the Aegean Bronze age, 1939-1989.* Amsterdam: J.C.Gieben, 209-215.

Pappas, 2011: Παππάς, Β. 2011: *Γεωγραφικά Συστήματα Πληροφοριών και σχεδιασμός του χώρου.* Πάτρα: Εκδόσεις Πανεπιστημίου Πατρών.

Pappas, V. 1994: Developing Urban Information systems in Greece. A comparative approach and methodological issues. *Proceedings, 5th EGIS/MARI, Paris.*

Pappas, V. 2006: Small metropolitan areas in rapid transition: the case of Patras. *46th Congress of the European Regional Science Association "Enlargement, South Europe and Mediterranean"* Volos 30/8-3/9/2006.

Patterson, T.C. 1990: Some theoretical tensions within and between the processual and post-processual archaeologies. *Journal of Anthropological Archaeology 9/2,* 189-200.

Pearce, J. 2000: Techniques for Defining School Catchment Areas for Comparison with Census Data. *Computers, Environment and Urban Systems 24/4,* 283-303.

Peña, J.A., J.A. Esquivel, A. Ramos, M. del Mar Osuna & E. Rull, 1999: Data analysis of a magnetic survey to contrast the most common treatments of data procedures in shallow archaeological surveys. Barceló, J. A., I. Briz & A. Vila (eds): *New techniques for old times – CAA 98 – Computer Applications and Quantitative Methods in Archaeology: Proceedings of the 26th conference, Barcelona, March 1998.* Oxford: BAR Publishing, 41-46.

Peregrine, P.N. 1995: Networks of Power: The Mississippian World-System. Nassaney, M. (ed.): *Native American Interactions: Multiscalar Analyses and Interpretations.* Knoxville: University of Tenessee Press, 247-267.

Peskarin, S. 2002: GIS contribution to urban history and to the reconstruction of ancient landscape. Burenhult, G. (ed.): *Archaeological Informatics: Pushing the Envelope CAA2001. Computer Applications and Quantitative Methods in Archaeology.* Oxford: BAR Publishing - BAR International Series 1016, 125-128.

Petrakos & Oikonomou, 1999: Πετράκος, Γ. & Δ. Οικονόμου, 1999: Διεθνοποίηση και διαρθρωτικές αλλαγές στο ευρωπαϊκό σύστημα αστικών κέντρων. Οικονόμου, Δ. & Γ. Πετράκος (επιμ.): *Η ανάπτυξη των ελληνικών πόλεων: Διεπιστημονικές προσεγγίσεις αστικής ανάλυσης και πολιτικής.* Βόλος: Πανεπιστημιακές εκδόσεις Θεσσαλίας- Gutenberg, 13-44.

Philippides, 2005: Φιλιππίδης, Δ. 2005: Ο μεγάλος ασθενής. *Θέματα Χώρου και Τεχνών 36*, 53-56.

Pickard, R. (ed.) 2001: *Management of historic centres.* London: Spon Press.

Polydorides et al. 1985: Πολυδωρίδης, Ν., Χ. Βόσσος, Μ. Καρανικολάου, Β. Παππάς, Χ. Τριανταφύλλου & Δ. Τσαμαδιάς, 1985: *Η αξία γης στον αστικό χώρο, Θέματα Προγραμματισμού 9.* Αθήνα: Κέντρο Προγραμματισμού και Οικονομικών Ερευνών.

Premo, L.S. 2004: Local Spatial Autocorrelation Statistics quantify multi-scale patterns in distributional data: an example from the Maya Lowlands. *Journal of Archaeological Science, 31/7*, 855-866.

Raftopoulou, 1998: Ραυτοπούλου, Σ. Π. 1998: Οι δυνατότητες επιστημονικής έρευνας σ' εκείνες τις πόλεις που βρίσκονται κάτω από σύγχρονες, Συλλογικός τόμος: *Νέες πόλεις πάνω σε παλιές, επιστημονικό συνέδριο, Ρόδος 27-30 Σεπτεμβρίου 1993.* Ρόδος: ICOMOS – ΚΒ΄ ΕΠΚΑ – 4ᴴ ΕΒΑ – ΤΕΕ ΤΜΗΜΑ ΔΩΔΕΚΑΝΗΣΟΥ, 425-432.

Renfrew, C. & E.V. Level, 1979: Exploring Dominance: Predicting Polities from Centers. Renfrew, C. & K.L. Cooke (eds): *Transformations: mathematical Approaches to Culture Change.* New York: Academic Press, 145-167.

Renfrew, C. & P. Bahn, 1991: *Archaeology: Theories, Methods, and Practice.* London: Thames and Hudson.

Richards, J.D. 1998: Recent trends in computer applications in archeology. *Journal of Archaeological Research 6/4*, 331-382.

Rizakis, T. & M. Petropoulos, 2005: Ancient Patrai. Sklavenitis, T.E. & K.S. Staikos (eds): *Patras: from ancient times to the present.* Athens: Kotinos Editions SA, 2-55.

Robinson J. & E. Zubrow, 1999: Between spaces: Interpolation in archaeology. Gillings M., D. Mattingly & J. van Dalen (eds): *Geographical Information Systems and Landscape Archaeology.* Oxford: Oxbow Books, 65-83.

Robinson, W.S. 1951: A method for chronologically ordering archaeological deposits. *American Antiquity XVI/4*, 293-301.

Rodier, X., L. Saligny, B. Lefebvre & J. Pouliot, 2010: ToToPI (Topographie de Tours Pré-Industriel), a GIS for Understanding Urban Dynamics Based on the OH_ FET Model (Social Use, Space, and Time). Frischer, B., J. Webb Crawford & D. Koller (eds.): *Making History Interactive. Computer Applications and Quantitative Methods in Archaeology (CAA). Proceedings of the 37th International Conference, Williamsburg, Virginia, United States of America, March 22-26.* Oxford: BAR Publishing - BAR International Series S2079, 337-349.

Rua, H. 2009: Geographical information systems in archaeological analysis: a predictive model in the detection of rural Roman villae. *Journal of Archaeological Science 36*, 224-235.

Ruggles, A.J. & R.L. Church, 1996: Spatial Allocation in Archaeology: An Opportunity for Reevaluation. Maschner, H.D.G. (ed.): *New Methods Old Problems; Geographic Information Systems in Modern Archaeological Research.* Carbondale: Southern Illinois University Center for Archaeological Investigations, 147-173.

Runz de, C., E. Desjardin, F. Piantoni & M. Herbin, 2007: Management of multi-modal data using the Fuzzy Hough Transform: application to archaeological simulation. Ouarzazate, M., C. Rolland, O. Pastor & J.L Cavarero (eds): *First IEEE International Conference on Research Challenges in Information Sciences*, 351-356.

Sakellaridou, 1999: Σακελλαρίδου, Ρ. 1999: Το νέο κτήριο. Συλλογικός τόμος: *Το νέο κτήριο Διοικήσεως: Από την κατοικία του Γεωργίου Σταύρου στο επιτελικό κέντρο του Ομίλου της Εθνικής Τράπεζας.* Αθήνα: Ιστορικό Αρχείο Εθνικής Τραπέζης της Ελλάδος, 19-32.

Sarantakou, 2000: Σαραντάκου, Ε. 2000: Διερεύνηση του ιστορικού χαρακτήρα στον αστικό ιστό – Ανάπλαση στην παλαιά πόλη της Μυτιλήνης. Αυγερινού – Κολώνια, Σ. (επιμ.): *Νέες πόλεις πάνω σε παλιές: Το παράδειγμα της Σπάρτης, Επιστημονικό συνέδριο Σπάρτη 18-20 Φεβρουαρίου 1994.* Σπάρτη: Δήμος Σπάρτης – ICOMOS – TEE, 311-321.

Savage, S.H. 1990: Modelling the Late Archaic Social landscape. Allen, K.M.S., S.W. Green & E.B.W. Zubrow (eds): *Interpreting Space: GIS and archaeology.* London: Taylor & Francis, 330-355.

Schauman Lönnqvist, M. 2007: Rescue archaeology in Finland – Goals and practices. Bozoki Ernyey, K. (ed.): *European Preventive Archaeology: Papers of the EPAC*

Meeting, Vilnius 2004. Hungary – Council of Europe -National Office of Cultural Heritage, 50-56.

Schlader, R. 2002: Archaeological databases: what are they and what do they mean? Burenhult, G. (ed.): *Archaeological Informatics: Pushing the Envelope CAA2001. Computer Applications and Quantitative Methods in Archaeology.* Oxford: BAR Publishing - BAR International Series 1016, 517-520.

Schnapp, A. 1996: *The discovery of the past.* London: British Museum Press.

Schwarz, K.R. & J. Mount, 2006: Integrating spatial statistics into archaeological data modeling. Mehrer, W. & K. L. Westcott (eds): *GIS and Archaeological Site Location Modeling.* Boca Raton: Taylor & Francis, 167-189.

Semeraro, G. 1993: The excavation archive: an integrated system for the management of cartographic and alphanumeric data. Andresen, J., T. Madsen & I. Scollar (eds): *Computing the past: computer applications and quantitative methods in archaeology CAA92.* Århus: Århus University Press, 205-211.

Shanks, M. & C. Tilley 1994: *Re-Constructing Archaeology: theory and practice,* 2nd ed. London - N. York: Routledge.

Shennan S. 1988: *Quantifying Archaeology.* Edinburgh: Edinburgh University Press.

Sidiropoulos, G. & A. Sideris, 2003: Requirements and assumptions in visualization process of urban and surrounding areas (The case study of the Greek city in time). Doerr, M. & A. Sarris (eds): *CAA 2002: The digital heritage of archaeology.* Athens: Archive of Monuments and Publications, 63-68.

Simoni, H. & K. Papagiannopoulos, 1998: Project for the topography of ancient Achaia, Greece: Quantitative analysis and visualization of the results of the intensive surface survey at Kamenitsa. Peterson, J. (ed.): *The use of Geographic Information Systems in the study of ancient landscapes and features related to ancient land use.* European Commission: COST ACTION G2, 43-55.

Simoni, H. & K. Papagiannopoulos, 2001: Can schoolchildren digitize their history? Stančič, Z. & T. Veljanovski (eds): *Computing Archaeology for Understanding the Past CAA2000. Computer Applications and Quantitative Methods in Archaeology.* Oxford: BAR Publishing - BAR International Series 931, 363-368.

Simoni, H. 1999: The Geographical Information Systems in Cultural Resource Management, *Dialogues d' Histoire Ancienne 25/1,* 222-233.

Simoni, H. 2013: Archaeological Evaluation of Ground Disturbance Sites in Modern Greek Cities. Contreras, F., M. Farjas & F.J. Melero F.J.(eds): *CAA 2010: Fusion of Cultures. Proceedings of the 38th Annual Conference on Computer Applications and Quantitative Methods in Archaeology.* Oxford: BAR, 193-199.

Simoni, H. 2014: Multiple cultural strata and one urban identity: challenges and opportunities in Patras, Greece. Burdusel, E.-N., O. Matiu, D. Preda & A. Tomus (eds): *Cultural Encounters: The mosaic of urban identities. Proceedings of the 7th Annual Interdisciplinary Conference of the University Network of the European Capitals of Culture, Marseille 17-18th October 2013.* Sibiu: Lucian Blaga University of Sibiu Press, 97-111.

Sklavenitis, T.E. & K.S. Staikos (eds) 2005: *Patras: from ancient times to the present.* Athens: Kotinos Editions SA.

Skouris & Trova, 2003: Σκουρής, Π. & Ε. Τροβά, 2003: *Προστασία Αρχαιοτήτων και Πολιτιστικής Κληρονομιάς.* Αθήνα: Σάκκουλα.

Soetens, S., A. Sarris, K. Vansteenhuyse & S. Topouzi, 2003: GIS Variations on a Cretan Theme: Minoan Peak Sanctuaries. *Proceedings of the 9th International Aegean Conference, April 18-21 2002.* New Haven: Yale University, *www.ims.forth.gr/docs/metron2002B* (10-2-2010).

Spaulding, A.C. 1953: Statistical techniques for the discovery of artifact types. *American Antiquity XVIII/4,* 305-313.

Stančič, Z. & K.L. Kvamme, 1999: Settlement modeling through Boolean overlays of social and environmental variables. Barceló, J. A., I. Briz & A. Vila (eds): *New Techniques for Old Times CAA98. Computer Applications and Quantitative Methods in Archaeology.* Oxford: BAR Publishing, 231-237.

Stavropoulou Gatsi et al, 2006: Σταυροπούλου Γάτση, Μ., Γ. Αλεξοπούλου, Γ. Γεωργοπούλου & Α. Γκαδόλου, 2006: Το έργο των σωστικών ανασκαφών στην πόλη των Πατρών και την ευρύτερη περιοχή της: Νεότερα πολεοδομικά και τοπογραφικά στοιχεία. Συλλογικός τόμος: *Πρακτικά Α' Αρχαιολογικής Συνόδου Νότιας και Δυτικής Ελλάδας,* Ιούνιος 9-12 2006. Αθήνα: Τ.Α.Π., 81-100.

Stavropoulou Gatsi, 2001: Σταυροπούλου Γάτση Μ. 2001: Ο οικισμός της Εποχής του Χαλκού στην Παγώνα της Πάτρας. Mitsopoulos Leon, V. (επιμ.): *Forschungen in der Peloponnes.* Athen: Österreichisches Archäologisches Institut, 29-38.

Stillwell, J. & G. Clarke (eds) 2004: *Applied GIS & spatial analysis.* Chichester: Wiley.

Stillwell, J., S. Geertman & S. Openshaw (eds) 1999: *Geographical information and planning.* Berlin, New York: Springer.

Syllaios et al 2007: Συλλαίος, Ν., Ι. Γήτας & Γ. Συλλαίος, 2007: *Εισαγωγή στα Γεωγραφικά Συστήματα Πληροφοριών και στην τηλεπισκόπηση.* Θεσσαλονίκη: εκδ. Γιαχούδη.

Thapar, N., D. Wong & J. Lee 1999: The changing geography of population centroids in the United States between 1970 and 1980. *The Geographical Bulletin 41/1*, 45-56.

Theorema, 2007: Θεώρημα Α.Ε. Σύμβουλοι Ανάπτυξης, 2007: Μέρος ΑΙ- Χωροταξική και πολεοδομική αναγνώριση. *Μελέτη Ρυθμιστικού Σχεδίου και Προγράμματος Προστασίας Περιβάλλοντος οικιστκού συγκροτήματος Πάτρας Α' φάση*. Αθήνα: ΥΠΕΧΩΔΕ Διεύθυνση Πολεοδομικού Σχεδιασμού.

Theorema, 2009: Θεώρημα Α.Ε. Σύμβουλοι Ανάπτυξης, 2009: *Μελέτη Ρυθμιστικού Σχεδίου και Προγράμματος Προστασίας Περιβάλλοντος οικιστκού συγκροτήματος Πάτρας Β' φάση*. Αθήνα: ΥΠΕΧΩΔΕ Διεύθυνση Πολεοδομικού Σχεδιασμού.

Thomas, R.M. 2007: Development-led archaeology in England. Bozoki Ernyey, K. (ed.): *European Preventive Archaeology: Papers of the EPAC Meeting, Vilnius 2004*. Hungary – Council of Europe -National Office of Cultural Heritage, 33-42.

Tobler, W. 1970: A computer movie simulating urban growth in the Detroit region. *Economic Geography, 46/2*, 234-240.

Tomlinson, R.F., D.F. Marble & H.W. Calkins 1976: *Computer Handling of Geographic data, UNESCO Natural Resource Research Series, no 13*. Paris: The UNESCO Press.

Triantafyllos, 2004: Τριαντάφυλλος, Δ. 2004: Η ΙΘ' Εφορεία Προϊστορικών και Κλασικών Αρχαιοτήτων και τα μεγάλα έργα. Μπακιρτζής, Χ. (επιμ.): *Αρχαιολογικές έρευνες και μεγάλα δημόσια έργα. Αρχαιολογική συνάντηση Εργασίας, Επταπύργιο 18-20 Σεπτεμβρίου 2003*. Αθήνα: Υπουργείο Πολιτισμού, Επιτροπή Παρακολούθησης Μεγάλων Έργων, 187-188.

Tsilipakou, 2004: Τσιλιπάκου, Α. 2004: Παρεμβάσεις σχετικά με τον προβληματισμό επί των έργων Μπακιρτζής, Χ. (επιμ.): *Αρχαιολογικές έρευνες και μεγάλα δημόσια έργα. Αρχαιολογική συνάντηση Εργασίας, Επταπύργιο 18-20 Σεπτεμβρίου 2003*. Αθήνα: Υπουργείο Πολιτισμού, Επιτροπή Παρακολούθησης Μεγάλων Έργων, 427-430.

Tsokas, G.N., A. Giannopoulos, P. Tsourlos, G. Vargemezis, J.M. Tealby, A. Sarris, C.B. Papazachos & T. Savopoulou, 1994: A large scale geophysical survey in the archaeological site of Europos (northern Greece). *Journal of Applied Geophysics 32*, 85-98.

Vafidis, A., N. Economou & A. Sarris, 2003: Geophysical data presentation using GIS. Doerr, M. & A. Sarris (eds): *CAA 2002: The digital heritage of archaeology*. Athens: Archive of Monuments and Publications, 195-200.

Vaiou et al 2000: Βαΐου Ντ., Μ. Μαντουβάλου και Μ. Μαυρίδου, 2000: Η μεταπολεμική Ελληνική πολεοδομία μεταξύ θεωρίας και συγκυρίας. Δέφνερ Α. (επιμ.): *Η Πολεοδομία στην Ελλάδα από το 1949 έως το 1974*. Βόλος: Τμήμα Μηχανικών Χωροταξίας και

Περιφερειακής Ανάπτυξης – Πανεπιστήμιο Θεσσαλίας, 25-37.

van Dyke Robinson, E. 1912: Review of: Influences of Geographic Environment; on the Basis of Ratzel's System of Anthropo-Geography. *The American Economic Review 2/2*, 338-340.

van Leusen, M., A.R. Millard & B. Ducke, 2009: Dealing with uncertainty in archaeological prediction. Kamermans, H., M. van Leusen & P.Verhagen, (eds): *Archaeological Prediction and Risk Management: alternatives to current practice*. Leiden: Leiden University Press, 123-160.

van Leusen, P.M. 1996: GIS and locational modeling in Dutch archaeology: a review of current approaches. Maschner, H.D.G. (ed.): *New Methods Old Problems; Geographic Information Systems in Modern Archaeological Research*. Carbondale: Southern Illinois University Center for Archaeological Investigations, 177-197.

Varvitsiotis, 2005: Βαρβιτσιώτης, I.M. 2005: *Πολιτιστική φωτογραμμετρία*. Αθήνα: Μίλητος.

Veljanovski, T. & Z. Stančič 2006: Predictive modeling in archaeological location analysis and archaeological resource management: Principles and applications. Mehrer, W. & K. L. Westcott (eds): *GIS and Archaeological Site Location Modeling*. Boca Raton: Taylor & Francis, 393-411.

Verhagen, P. 2009: Predictive models put to test. Kamermans, H., M. van Leusen & Ph. Verhagen (eds): *Archaeological Prediction and Risk Management: alternatives to current practice*. Leiden: Leiden University Press, 71-122.

Verhoeven, G. & F. Vermeulen, 2004: The Potenza valley survey: towards an explanation of the settlement patterns through the combined use of GIS and different survey techniques. Ausserer, K.F., W. Börner, M. Goriany & L. Karlhuber-Vöckl (eds): *Enter the Past. The E-way into the four Dimensions of Cultural Heritage. CAA 2003, Computer Applications and Quantitative Methods in Archaeology*. Oxford: BAR Publishing - BAR International Series 1227, 312-316.

Vingopoulou I. 2005: Patrae, Patrasso, Patras... A town from history to micro-histories. The accounts of the foreign travellers (16th-early 20th century). Sklavenitis, T.E. & K.S. Staikos (eds): *Patras: from ancient times to the present*. Athens: Kotinos Editions SA, 212-245.

Vullo, N., F. Fontana & A. Guerreschi, 1999: The application of GIS to intra-site spatial analysis: preliminary results from Alpe Veglia (Vb) and Mondeval de Sora (BL), two Mesolithic sites in the Italian Alps. Barceló, J. A., I. Briz & A. Vila (eds): New techniques for old times – CAA 98 – Computer Applications and Quantitative Methods in Archaeology: Proceedings of the 26th conference, Barcelona, March 1998. Oxford, BAR Publishing, 111- 115

Wansleeben, M. & L.B.M. Verhart, 1995: GIS on different spatial levels and the Neolithization process in the south-eastern Netherlands. Lock, G. & Z. Stančič (eds): *Archaeology and Geographical Information Systems: a European Agenda.* London: Taylor & Francis, 153-169.

Warren, R.E. 1990: Predictive modelling of archaeological site location: a case study in the Midwest. Allen, K.M.S., S.W. Green & E.B.W. Zubrow (eds): *Interpreting Space: GIS and archaeology.* London: Taylor & Francis, 201-215.

Warren, R.E., S.G. Oliver, J.A. Ferguson & R.E. Druhot, 1987: *A predictive model of archaeological site location in the Western Shawnee National Forest, Technical report No. 86-262-17.* Springfield: Quaternary Studies Programm, Illinois State Museum.

Westcott K.L. & J.A. Kuiper, 2000: using a GIS to model prehistoric site distributions in the upper Chesapeake Bay. Westcott, K. L. & R. J. Brandon (eds): *Practical Applications of GIS for Archaeologists: A Predictive Modeling Toolkit.* London: Taylor & Francis, 59-72.

Westcott, K. L. & R. J. Brandon (eds) 2000: *Practical Applications of GIS for Archaeologists: A Predictive Modeling Toolkit.* London: Taylor & Francis.

Wheatley, D. & M. Gillings, 2002: *Spatial Technology and Archaeology: The Archaeological applications of GIS.* London: Taylor & Francis.

Wheatley, D. 1993: Going over old ground: GIS, archaeological theory and the act of perception. Andresen, J., T. Madsen & I. Scollar (eds): *Computing the past: computer applications and quantitative methods in archaeology CAA92.* Århus: Århus University Press, 133-138.

Whitley, T.G. 2004: Causality and cross-purposes in archaeological predictive modeling. Ausserer, K.F., W. Börner, M. Goriany & L. Karlhuber-Vöckl, (eds): *Enter the Past. The E-way into the four Dimensions of Cultural Heritage. CAA 2003, Computer Applications and Quantitative Methods in Archaeology.* Oxford: BAR Publishing - BAR Int. Series 1227, 236-239.

Wilcox, B., 2012: Archaeological Predictive Modelling Used For Cultural Heritage Management. Zhou, M., I. Romanowska, Z. Wu, P. Xu & P. Verhagen (eds.): *Revive the Past. Computer Applications and Quantitative Methods in Archaeology (CAA). Proceedings of the 39th International Conference, Beijing, April 12-16 2011.* Amsterdam: Pallas Publications,. 353-358.

Wilcox, W. 2013: Transparency, Testing and Standards for Archaeological Predictive Modelling. Earl, G., T. Sly, A. Chrysanthi, P. Murrieta-Flores, C. Papadopoulos, I. Romanowska, & D. Wheatley (eds): *Archaeology in the Digital Era Papers from the 40th Annual Conference of Computer Applications and Quantitative Methods in Archaeology (CAA), Southampton, 26-29 March 2012.* Amsterdam, Amsterdam: University Press, 340-347.

Willems, W.J.H. 2008: Archaeological resource mamagement and preservation. Kars, H. & R.M. Heeringen (eds): *Preserving archaeological remains in situ. Proceedings of the 3rd Conference 2006 Amsterdam.* Amsterdam: Institute for Geo- and Bioarchaeology, 253-260.

Wiseman J. & K. Zachos (eds) 2003: *Landscape archaeology in southern Epirus, Greece I.* Hesperia Supplement 32: The American School of Classical Studies at Athens.

Wylie, A. 1993: A proliferation of new archaeologists: Beyond objectivism and relativism. Yoffee, N. & A. Sherratt (eds): *Archaeological theory: who sets the agenda?* Cambridge: Cambridge University Press, 20-26.

Yerolympos, 2000: Γερόλυμπου Καραδήμου, A. 2000: Ο ΓΟΚ και η ελληνική πόλη: Από τη συνολική πολεοδομική αντίληψη στη ρύθμιση της ιδιωτικής κερδοσκοπίας. Δέφνερ, A. (επιμ.): *Η Πολεοδομία στην Ελλάδα από το 1949 έως το 1974.* Βόλος: Τμήμα Μηχανικών Χωροταξίας και Περιφερειακής Ανάπτυξης – Πανεπιστήμιο Θεσσαλίας, 151-165.

Yerolympos, A. 1996: *Urban Transformations in the Balkans (1820-1920): Aspects of Balkan Town Planning and the remaking of Thessaloniki.* Thessaloniki: University Studio Press.

Yialouri, 2010: Γιαλούρη, E. 2010: Η δυναμική των μνημείων: Αναζητήσεις στο πεδίο της μνήμης και της λήθης. Γιαννακόπουλος, K. & Γ. Γιαννιτσιώτης (επιμ.): *Αμφισβητούμενοι χώροι στην πόλη: Χωρικές προσεγγίσεις του πολιτισμού.* Αθήνα: Αλεξάνδρεια, 349-380.

Yoffee, N. & A. Sherratt, 1993: Introduction: the sources of archaeological theory. Yoffee, N. & A. Sherratt (eds): *Archaeological theory: who sets the agenda?* Cambridge: Cambridge University Press, 1-9.

Zarifis, 1998: Ζαρίφης, N. 1998: Συμβολή της Πληροφορικής στην τεκμηρίωση, τη μελέτη και τον προγραμματισμό επεμβάσεων σε ιστορικά κέντρα: Το παράδειγμα της Ρόδου. Συλλογικός τόμος: *Νέες πόλεις πάνω σε παλιές, Επιστημονικό Συνέδριο, Ρόδος 27-30 Σεπτεμβρίου 1993.* Ρόδος: ICOMOS – ΚΒ΄ ΕΠΚΑ – 4ᴴ ΕΒΑ – ΤΕΕ ΤΜΗΜΑ ΔΩΔΕΚΑΝΗΣΟΥ, 623-633.

Zarifis, N. & D. Brokou, 2002: GIS and space analysis in the study of the Hospitallers' fortifications in the Dodecanese. Burenhult, G. (ed.): Archaeological Informatics: Pushing the Envelope CAA2001. Computer Applications and Quantitative Methods in Archaeology. Oxford: BAR Publishing - BAR International Series 1016, 149-153.

Zarifis, N. 1996: Towards a computer information system for the archaeological sites and for the monuments in Rhodes. *Archeologia e Calcolatori 7,* 809-819.

Zinglersen, K.B. 2004: Odense byGIS- Odense urban archaeological GIS. Ausserer, K.F., W. Börner, M.

Goriany & L. Karlhuber-Vöckl, (eds): *Enter the Past. The E-way into the four Dimensions of Cultural Heritage. CAA 2003, Computer Applications and Quantitative Methods in Archaeology*. Oxford: BAR Publishing - BAR International Series 1227, 147-150.

Zois, 1990: Ζώης, Α. 1990: *Η αρχαιολογία στην Ελλάδα: Πραγματικότητες και προοπτικές*. Αθήνα: Πολύτυπο.

Zubrow, E.B.W. & S.W. Green, 1990: Coping with space: commentary on data sources, hardware and software. Allen, K.M.S., S.W. Green & E.B.W. Zubrow (eds): *Interpreting Space: GIS and archaeology*. London: Taylor & Francis, 129-133.

Appendix

Extract from the Database

ID	SYNTEL ESTHS	MAXC OVER	MAXIPS OS	ADDRESS	OTNO	OWN ER	COST	MAXDE P FREE	MINDEP ARCH_ EXC	MAXD EP DIG	MINDEP DIG	ARCHAE OLOGY	APPLICATI ON
1	16	70	11,00	ΜΠΟΥΜΠΟ ΥΛΙΝΑΣ 67-69	181	Ι	2,00	0,58	0,58	9,00	9,00	1,00	20/10/2006
2	16	70	12,00	ΑΛ. ΥΨΗΛΑΝ	206	Ι	2,00	2,00		2,00	1,00	2,00	1/1/2000
3	16	70	12,00	ΜΙΑΟΥΛΗ 74	205	Ι	2,00	1,00	1,00	1,50	1,00	1,00	2/12/2004
4	16	70	12,00	ΤΣΑΜΑΔΟΥ ΄	208	Ι	2,00	0,80		0,80	0,80	2,00	1/1/2000
5	24	70	16,00	ΓΟΥΝΑΡΗ 24	221	Ι	2,00	1,00		1,00	1,00	2,00	1/1/2000
6	24	70	16,00	ΧΑΡΑΛΑΜΠΗ	232	Ι	2,00	2,00		2,00	1,50	2,00	1/1/2000
7	24	70	19,00	ΝΙΚΗΤΑ 40	235	Ι	1,00	1,00	1,00	3,50	3,50	1,00	20/2/2006
8	24	70	19,00	ΕΡΕΝΣΤΡΩΛ	235	Ι	2,00	3,00		3,00	3,00	2,00	1/1/2000
9	12	70	8,00	ΧΑΡΑΛΑΜΠΗ	461	Ι	2,00	1,50		1,50	1,50	2,00	1/1/2000
10				ΣΩΤΗΡΙΑΔΟ΄	464	Ι	2,00	3,00		3,00	2,00	2,00	1/1/2000
11	12	70	8,00	ΕΙΣΟΔΙΑ, ΔΕΙ	465	Ι	2,00	0,80		0,80	0,80	2,00	1/1/2000
12				ΠΑΛΑΙΟ ΝΟΣ	448	Κ	2,00	0,35	0,35	1,00	1,00	1,00	1/1/2000
13	12	70	8,00	ΝΕΟΦΥΤΟΥ	450	Ι	2,00	1,70		1,70	1,70	1,00	1/1/2000
14	12	70	8,00	ΠΑΛΙΟ ΝΟΣC	450	Ι	2,00	1,40	1,40	2,50	2,50	1,00	4/4/2005
15	21	70	12,00	ΣΩΤΗΡΙΑΔΟ Υ 43	455	Ι	2,00	9,00	9,00	9,00	9,00	1,00	3/8/2004
16	21	70	12,00	ΣΩΤΗΡΙΑΔΟ΄	455	Ι	2,00	0,20	0,20	2,50	2,50	1,00	22/11/2006
17	24	70	16,00	ΓΟΥΝΑΡΗ 93	457	Ι	2,00	2,50		4,00	4,00	1,00	1/1/2000
18	24	70	16,00	ΓΟΥΝΑΡΗ 95	457	Ι	2,00	1,80		1,80	1,80	1,00	1/1/2000
19	21	70	12,00	ΧΑΡΑΛΑΜΠΗ	457	Ι	2,00	0,00		0,00	0,00	2,00	1/1/2000
20	12	70	8,00	ΗΛ. ΜΗΝΙΑΤΙ	469	Ι	1,00	2,00	2,00	2,00	2,00	1,00	18/5/2006
21	12	70	8,00	ΑΓ. ΓΕΩΡΓΙΟ	470	Ι	2,00	1,00		1,00	1,00	2,00	1/1/2000
22	21	70	12,00	ΕΡΙΣΣΟΥ 22	474	Ι	2,00	1,20		1,20	1,20	2,00	1/1/2000
23	21	70	12,00	ΗΦΑΙΣΤΟΥ 3	476	Ι	2,00	9,00		9,00	9,00	2,00	1/1/2000
24	24	70	16,00	ΑΓ. ΝΙΚΟΛΑC	487	Ι	2,00	2,80		2,80	2,80	2,00	1/1/2000
25	24	70	16,00	ΚΑΝΑΚΑΡΗ 1	488	Ι	2,00	3,50	3,50	3,50	3,50	1,00	19/12/2006
26	24	70	16,00	ΕΡΜΟΥ 59 (Α	501	Ι	2,00	1,30		1,30	1,30	2,00	1/1/2000
27	24	70	16,00	ΕΡΜΟΥ 42	514	Ι	2,00	0,60		0,60	0,60	2,00	1/1/2000
28	24	70	16,00	ΕΡΜΟΥ 45-4΄	515	Ι	2,00	1,50		1,50	1,50	2,00	1/1/2000
29	24	70	16,00	ΕΡΜΟΥ 9-11	516	Ι	2,00	0,30		0,30	0,30	2,00	1/1/2000
30	24	70	16,00	ΠΑΝΤΑΝΑΣΣ	519	Ι	2,00	2,20		2,20	2,20	2,00	1/1/2000
31	16	70	11,00	ΑΓΟΡΑ ΑΡΓΥ	551	Κ	2,00	1,00		1,00	1,00	2,00	1/1/2000
32	24	70	16,00	ΖΑΪΜΗ 48-50	555	Ι	2,00	1,00	1,00	1,00	1,00	1,00	23/9/2005
33	24	70	16,00	ΖΑΪΜΗ 56	556	Ι	2,00	1,80		1,80	1,80	2,00	1/1/2000
34	24	70	16,00	ΖΑΙΜΗ 71	568	Ι	2,00	1,30		1,30	1,30	2,00	1/1/2000
35	21	70	12,00	ΖΑΙΜΗ 81-83	565	Ι	2,00	3,00		3,00	2,00	2,00	1/1/2000
36	24	70	19,00	ΚΟΡΙΝΘΟΥ 3	648	Ι	2,00	3,00		3,00	3,00	2,00	1/1/2000
37	24	70	19,00	ΚΟΡΙΝΘΟΥ 8	618	Ι	2,00	3,50		3,50	3,50	2,00	1/1/2000
38	24	70	19,00	ΚΟΡΙΝΘΟΥ 4	641	Ι	2,00	1,50		1,50	1,50	2,00	1/1/2000
39	24	70	19,00	ΚΟΡΙΝΘΟΥ 1	620	Ι	2,00	0,70		0,70	0,70	2,00	1/1/2000
40	24	70	19,00	ΕΛΛΗΝΟΣ ΣΊ	632	Ι	2,00	1,50		1,50	1,50	2,00	1/1/2000
41	24	70	19,00	ΓΙΑΝΝΙΤΣΩΝ	653	Ι	2,00	3,00		3,00	1,60	2,00	1/1/2000

Tables of statistical tests

TABLE 1: Observed number of excavations in the buildable and unbuildable zones and the expected number in a uniform distribution, based on the surface area of each zone.

	SURFACE (cells)	*OBSERVED EXCAVATIONS*	*EXPECTED EXCAVATIONS*
UNBUILDABLE	20405	703	793
BUILDABLE	3961	244	154
TOTAL	24366	947	947

x^2 test (α=0.05): p<0.0001 p<α **NULL HYPOTHESIS DISPROVED**

TABLE 2: Observed number of excavations in the different zones of f.a.r. and the expected number in a uniform distribution, based on the surface area of each zone.

	SURFACE (cells)	*OBSERVED EXCAVATIONS*	*EXPECTED EXCAVATIONS*
LOW f.a.r.	10666	216	415
MEDIUM f.a.r.	6333	194	246
HIGH f.a.r.	3406	293	132
UNBUILDABLE	3961	244	154
TOTAL	24366	947	947

x^2 test (α=0.05): p= 2.34696E-76 p<α **NULL HYPOTHESIS DISPROVED**

TABLE 3: Observed number of archaeological excavations in the buildable and unbuildable zones and the expected number in a uniform distribution, based on the surface area of each zone.

	SURFACE (cells)	*OBSERVED ARCHAEOLOGICAL EXCAVATIONS*	*EXPECTED ARCHAEOLOGICAL EXCAVATIONS*
BUILDABLE	20405	90	123
UNBUILDABLE	3961	57	24
TOTAL	24366	147	147

x^2 test (α=0.05): p<0.0001 p<α **NULL HYPOTHESIS DISPROVED**

TABLE 4: Observed number of archaeological excavations in the different zones of f.a.r. and the expected number in a uniform distribution, based on the surface area of each zone.

	SURFACE (cells)	*OBSERVED ARCHAEOLOGICAL EXCAVATIONS*	*EXPECTED ARCHAEOLOGICAL EXCAVATIONS*
LOW f.a.r.	10666	14	64
MEDIUM f.a.r.	6333	20	38
HIGH f.a.r.	3406	56	21
UNBUILDABLE	3961	57	24
TOTAL	24366	147	147

x^2 test (α=0.05): p=2.10119E-33 p<α **NULL HYPOTHESIS DISPROVED**

TABLE 5: Observed proportion of the surface by chronological period in the buildable and unbuildable zones and the expected proportion in a uniform distribution, based on the surface area of each zone.

	BUILDABLE observed % surface	*UNBUILDABLE* observed % surface	*Expected % surface*
CLASSICAL/HELLENISTIC	13	3	10
ROMAN	53	76	61
BYZANTINE	19	9	15
UNKNOWN	15	12	14
TOTAL	100	100	100
x^2 test (α=0.05)	p=0.3821162 $p>\alpha$ **NULL HYPOTHESIS TRUE**	p= 0.0127 $p<\alpha$ **NULL HYPOTHESIS DISPROVED**	

TABLE 6: Observed proportion of the surface by chronological period in the different zones of m.p.h. and the expected proportion in a uniform distribution, based on the surface area of each zone.

	LOW m.p.h. observed % surface	*MEDIUM m.p.h.* observed % surface	*HIGH m.p.h.* observed % surface	*UNBUILDABLE* observed % surface	*Expected % surface*
CLASS./HELLEN.	15	5	14	3	9
ROMAN	44	52,5	45	76	56
BYZANTINE	22	12,5	18	9	14
POSTBYZANTINE	15	17,5	5	0	8
UNKNOWN	4	12,5	18	12	13
TOTAL	100	100	100	100	100
x^2 test (α=0.05)	p<0.0001 $p<\alpha$ **NULL HYPOTHESIS DISPROVED**	p=0.0059 $p<\alpha$ **NULL HYPOTHESIS DISPROVED**	p=0.0506 $p<\alpha$ **NULL HYPOTHESIS DISPROVED**	p=0.0005 $p<\alpha$ **NULL HYPOTHESIS DISPROVED**	

TABLE 7: Observed proportion of the surface by chronological period in the different zones of f.a.r. and the expected proportion in a uniform distribution, based on the surface area of each zone.

	LOW f.a.r. observed % surface	*MEDIUM f.a.r.* observed % surface	*HIGH f.a.r.* observed % surface	*Expected % surface*
CLASS./HELLEN.	0	13	12	9
ROMAN	78	45	45	56
BYZANTINE	11	19	17	14
POSTBYZANTINE	0	16	10	8
UNKNOWN	11	7	16	13
TOTAL	100	100	100	100
x^2 test (α=0.05)	p<0.0001 $p<\alpha$ **NULL HYPOTHESIS DISPROVED**	p=0.0029 $p<\alpha$ **NULL HYPOTHESIS DISPROVED**	p=0.199 $p>\alpha$ **NULL HYPOTHESIS TRUE**	

TABLE 8: Observed and expected numbers of types of finds in the buildable and unbuildable zones.

| | BUILDABLE | | UNBUILDABLE | | TOTAL |
	observed	expected	observed	expected	observed
MOVABLE	82	86	49	45	131
STANDING	61	49	13	25	74
WORKSHOPS	6	5	1	2	7
GRAVES	15	10	1	6	16
INFRASTRUCTURE	30	44	37	23	67
TOTAL	194		101		295
x^2 test (α=0.05)	p= 0.038 p<α **NULL HYPOTHESIS DISPROVED**		p= 0.0006 p<α **NULL HYPOTHESIS DISPROVED**		

TABLE 9: Observed and expected proportion of surface by type of finds in the different zones of m.p.h., based on the surface area of each zone.

	LOW m.p.h. observed % surface	*MEDIUM m.p.h.* observed % surface	*HIGH m.p.h.* observed % surface	*Expected % surface*
MOVABLE	43	38	45	45
STANDING	35	35	25	25
WORKSHOPS	2	5	3	2
GRAVES	4	3	15	5
INFRASTRUCTURE	16	19	12	23
TOTAL	100	100	100	100
x^2 test (α=0.05)	p=0.144 p>α **NULL HYPOTHESIS TRUE**	p=0.0758 p>α **NULL HYPOTHESIS TRUE**	p=0.0003 p<α **NULL HYPOTHESIS DISPROVED**	

TABLE 10: Observed proportion of the surface by type of preservation status of antiquities in the buildable and unbuildable zones and the expected proportion in a uniform distribution, based on the surface area of each zone.

	BUILDABLE observed % surface	*UNBUILDABLE* observed % surface	*Expected % surface*
DECONSTRUCTION	31	7	23
REBURIAL	36	63	45
REMOVAL	25	3	17
UNKNOWN	8	27	15
TOTAL	100	100	100
x^2 test (α=0.05)	p=0.012245 p<α **NULL HYPOTHESIS DISPROVED**	p<0.0001 p<α **NULL HYPOTHESIS DISPROVED**	

TABLE 11: Observed proportion of the surface by type of preservation status of antiquities in the different zones of f.a.r. and the expected proportion in a uniform distribution, based on the surface area of each zone.

	LOW f.a.r. % surface	*MEDIUM f.a.r.* % surface	*HIGH f.a.r.* % surface	*Expected % surface*
DECONSTRUCTION	35	31	30	23
REBURIAL	35	46	32	45
REMOVAL	24	15	29	17
UNKNOWN	6	8	9	15
TOTAL	100	100	100	100
x^2 test (α=0.05)	p=0.0008835 p<α **NULL HYPOTHESIS DISPROVED**	p=0.0950119 p>α **NULL HYPOTHESIS TRUE**	p=0.00153 p<α **NULL HYPOTHESIS DISPROVED**	

TABLE 12: Observed size of potential archaeological and potential non-archaeological surfaces in the buildable and unbuildable zones and the expected size in a uniform distribution, based on the surface area of each zone.

	BUILDABLE (cells)		UNBUILDABLE (cells)	
	Observed	Expected	Observed	Expected
Potential archaeological surface	1302	1282	61	81
Potential non-archaeolog. surface	18925	18945	1210	1190
TOTAL	20227		1271	
x² test (α=0.05)	p= 0.572039 p>α **NULL HYPOTHESIS TRUE**		p= 0.024188 p<α **NULL HYPOTHESIS DISPROVED**	

TABLE 13: Observed size of potential archaeological and potential non-archaeological surfaces in the different zones of f.a.r. and the expected size in a uniform distribution, based on the surface area of each zone.

	LOW f.a.r. (cells)		*MEDIUM f.a.r. (cells)*		*HIGH f.a.r. (cells)*	
	Observed	Expected	Observed	Expected	Observed	Expected
Potential archaeological surface	304	666	338	401	660	216
Potential non-archaeolog. surface	10200	9838	5980	5917	2745	3189
TOTAL	10504		6318		3405	
x² test (α=0.05)	p<0.0001 p<α **NULL HYPOTHESIS DISPROVED**		p=0.0014 p<α **NULL HYPOTHESIS DISPROVED**		p<0.0001 p<α **NULL HYPOTHESIS DISPROVED**	

TABLE 14: Descriptive statistics and results of the Mann-Whitney test regarding the distribution of intended excavation depths in the excavations in the buildable and unbuildable spaces.

	DESCRIPTIVE STATISTICS					MANN-WHITNEY
	Dataset size	*Mean*	*Median*	*Minimum*	*Maximum*	*RESULTS*
BUILDABLE	683	2.1	2.0	0.2	5.5	p= 0.6383
UNBUILDABLE	229	2.0	2.2	0.3	6.0	α=0.05 p>α **NULL HYPOTHESIS TRUE**

TABLE 15: Descriptive statistics and results of the Mann-Whitney test regarding the distribution of intended excavation depths in the archaeological excavations in the buildable and unbuildable spaces.

	DESCRIPTIVE STATISTICS					MANN-WHITNEY
	Dataset size	*Mean*	*Median*	*Minimum*	*Maximum*	*RESULTS*
BUILDABLE	76	2.4	2.5	0.2	5.5	p= 0.0000
UNBUILDABLE	42	0.9	0.8	0.3	4.0	α=0.05 p<α **NULL HYPOTHESIS DISPROVED**

TABLE 16: Descriptive statistics and results of the Mann-Whitney test regarding the distribution of intended excavation depths in the non-archaeological excavations in the buildable and unbuildable spaces.

	DESCRIPTIVE STATISTICS					MANN-WHITNEY
	Dataset size	*Mean*	*Median*	*Minimum*	*Maximum*	*RESULTS*
BUILDABLE	607	2.1	2.0	0.2	5.2	p= 0.0002
UNBUILDABLE	187	2.3	2.3	0.4	6.0	α=0.05 p<α **NULL HYPOTHESIS DISPROVED**

TABLE 17: Descriptive statistics and results of the Kruskall-Wallis test regarding the distribution of intended excavation depths in the archaeological excavations in the different zones of f.a.r.

	DESCRIPTIVE STATISTICS					KRUSKALL-WALLIS	
	Dataset size	*Mean*	*Median*	*Minimum*	*Maximum*	*Mean rank*	*Z*
Low f.a.r.	12	1.9	1.8	0.2	3.5	64.5	0.54
Medium f.a.r.	116	2.3	2.1	1	5.5	75.4	2.00
High f.a.r.	48	2.5	2.9	0.3	4	81.8	5.86
Unbuildable	42	0.9	0.8	0.3	4	26.5	-7.79
	p= 0.000	α=0.05	p<α	**NULL HYPOTHESIS DISPROVED**			

TABLE 18: Descriptive statistics and results of the Kruskall-Wallis test regarding the distribution of intended excavation depths in the non-archaeological excavations in the different zones of f.a.r.

	DESCRIPTIVE STATISTICS					KRUSKALL-WALLIS	
	Dataset size	*Mean*	*Median*	*Minimum*	*Maximum*	*Mean rank*	*Z*
Low f.a.r.	201	1.9	2.0	0.2	5.0	333.9	-4.55
Medium f.a.r.	173	2.0	2.0	0.3	5.0	357.9	-2.57
High f.a.r.	233	2.3	2.5	0.3	5.2	437.5	3.17
Unbuildable	187	2.1	2.3	0.4	6.0	452.7	3.76
	p= 0.000	α=0.05	p<α	**NULL HYPOTHESIS DISPROVED**			

TABLE 19: Descriptive statistics and results of the Kruskall-Wallis test regarding the distribution of maximum known depth without archaeological deposits in the archaeological excavations in the different zones of f.a.r.

	DESCRIPTIVE STATISTICS					KRUSKALL-WALLIS	
	Dataset size	*Mean*	*Median*	*Minimum*	*Maximum*	*Mean rank*	*Z*
Low f.a.r.	14	1.5	1.3	0.2	3.5	77.1	1.15
Medium f.a.r.	20	1.2	1.0	0.0	2.5	69.0	0.38
High f.a.r.	54	1.3	1.2	0.05	3.5	72.5	1.65
Unbuildable	43	0.8	0.8	0.0	2.8	52.8	-2.78
	p= 0.044	α=0.05	p<α	**NULL HYPOTHESIS DISPROVED**			

TABLE 20: Descriptive statistics and results of the Mann-Whitney test regarding the distribution of maximum known depth without archaeological deposits in the archaeological excavations in the buildable and unbuildable spaces.

	DESCRIPTIVE STATISTICS					MANN-WHITNEY	
	Dataset size	*Mean*	*Median*	*Minimum*	*Maximum*	*RESULTS*	
BUILDABLE	88	1.3	1.2	0.0	3.5	p= 0.005	
UNBUILDABLE	43	0.8	0.8	0.0	2.8	α=0.05	
						p<α	
						NULL HYPOTHESIS DISPROVED	

TABLE 21: Descriptive statistics and results of the Kruskall-Wallis test regarding the distribution of maximum known depth without archaeological deposits in the non-archaeological excavations in the different zones of f.a.r.

	DESCRIPTIVE STATISTICS					KRUSKALL-WALLIS	
	Dataset size	*Mean*	*Median*	*Minimum*	*Maximum*	*Mean rank*	*Z*
Low f.a.r.	201	1.9	2.0	0.2	5.0	334.9	-4.51
Medium f.a.r.	173	2.0	2.0	0.3	5.0	358.9	-2.53
High f.a.r.	234	2.3	2.5	0.0	5.2	436.7	3.07
Unbuildable	187	2.3	2.3	0.4	6.0	453.7	3.79
	p= 0.000	α=0.05	p<α	**NULL HYPOTHESIS DISPROVED**			

TABLE 22: Descriptive statistics and results of the Mann-Whitney test regarding the distribution of maximum known depth without archaeological deposits in the non-archaeological excavations in the buildable and unbuildable spaces.

	DESCRIPTIVE STATISTICS					MANN-WHITNEY
	Dataset size	*Mean*	*Median*	*Minimum*	*Maximum*	*RESULTS*
BUILDABLE	608	2.1	2.0	0.0	5.2	p= 0.0001
UNBUILDABLE	187	2.3	2.3	0.4	6.0	α=0.05
						p<α
						NULL HYPOTHESIS DISPROVED

www.ingramcontent.com/pod-product-compliance
Lightning Source LLC
Chambersburg PA
CBHW061304270326
41932CB00029B/3468